Ma

A Winning Strategy

Corrected and Extended Edition for 2018/2019

by Martin Gruebele, Ph.D.
University of Illinois at Urbana-Champaign

and Gregory Scott, Ph.D.
California Polytechnic University at San Luis Obispo

with contributions from
Lana Pohlmann, Paul Ponder, Ed Scott, Julie Turner, Roy Tylinksi, Jay Yost and Harry K. Zink

ISBN 978-0-692-77538-7

© 2016 by Martin Gruebele and Gregory Scott
© 2017, 2018 corrected and updated editions

All rights reserved.

No part of this book may be reproduced or transmitted in any form or by any means, electronic or mechanical, without permission in writing from both authors. Permission may be sought by emailing the authors at mgruebel@illinois.edu and gscott02@calpoly.edu.

PREFACE

The Race Across America (RAAM) is effectively the World Cup of ultracycling. It spans 3000 miles from California to Maryland, and while no segment of it is grueling, the overall race unquestionably pushes the limits of human physical and mental endurance. Some of the finest ultracyclists in the world line up at the start. Only half to two thirds of them cross the finish line.

For 2018/2019, we have added a new Chapter 4, analyzing recent RAAM races and 'double-nap' strategies that split the sleep into a regular day and night period. We added a 12+ day race schedule of interest to Grandmasters[†] and women racers. Chapter 5 now discusses pre-race tapering in more detail, and additional information on topics such as night riding. Chapter 6 explains in more detail why 3 crews with 2 persons each is a recipe for success, and you'll find new equipment information in Chapter 7. A financial formula for RAAM with hotels is presented in Chapter 13. In addition, small errors and omissions were corrected.

In the 2016 race, three categories – Male Open, Female Open, and Male Masters[†] – were won by "rookies" against a field of experienced solo RAAM racers. While one might suppose that the "rookies" were freaks of nature, we suggest exactly the opposite: they were strong but not elite-level cyclists, who approached RAAM methodically, and rode a nearly optimal race to beat their equally strong competition. Strong legs are a fine starting point for an ultracycling win,[1] but rest strategy is even more important.

This book is sub-titled "A Winning Strategy," not "*The* Winning Strategy" for a good reason. There are several possible RAAM strategies for the Masters racer who wants to get to the front of the race, and the one that is best suited to a specific individual depends on preferred sleep patterns, organizational skills, and many other factors. The conventional strategy for Masters has been described by Keith Wolcott in his excellent book "One Million Pedal Strokes."

We adopted a less orthodox strategy for the race involving regular daytime sleep. This foreword asks three questions, so the reader can decide whether

---

[†] 'Open,' 'Masters' and 'Grandmasters' are our loose designations for the age groups used by RAAM, "Open"="under 50," "Masters"="50-59," "Grandmasters"="60-69."

our strategy might work for him or her. We wrote this book because it illustrates how a strategy different from the generally accepted one can win the Masters race. Our goal is not to provide you with a "Master Plan" (they always fail), but to make you think about race planning, sleep strategy, and flexible execution for your best performance in any multi-day endurance race. Hopefully you will find useful elements for your own strategy in this book.

The authors of this book are researchers. In the three-year preparation leading up to RAAM solo, our racer investigated the scientific endurance literature, past RAAM results and strategies, and repeatedly tested ideas himself. The approach of this book, "long daytime sleep – long nighttime ride" synthesizes that experience into a plan that was near-optimal for our racer. Each day, the Honey Badger (so we shall often call our racer Martin Gruebele, by the nickname his cycling buddies gave him years ago) slept about 4 hours in the middle of the day, and rode continuously for about 19 hours throughout the night. A 3-hour sleep period would not have worked, causing a drop-off in speed in the second half of the race. 5 hours would have been too much sleep, wasting precious time. There were no micro-rests, no scheduled stops other than crew exchanges. Yet the Honey Badger spent no more time in the saddle than the top three Male Open racers – he raced RAAM at the same average speed on the bike as the Open winner despite being 25 years older.

Our first question to the reader: Are you a person who can nap at any moment, anywhere? Or do you have a strong circadian rhythm, and take 15 or more minutes to fall asleep in bed? If you are the latter, the strategy in this book is indispensable for you. Our strategy of long daytime sleep breaks is a calculated risk, and not for the faint of heart. Getting to the front of the race requires patience for over a week, and if an extraordinarily strong rider – one of those freaks of nature – is among the field, you may never catch up to him or her.

Our second question to the reader: Are you a racer who likes to just ride and push hard, and go with the flow? Or can you stick to a seemingly easy schedule early on, when your body is telling you that you could do more? If you are the latter, the strategy in this book is indispensable for you. It emphasizes data analysis, planning, and execution, with the understanding that most people want to do too much early on, only to pay for it later. The situation must never get to that "pay later" stage if you want to do your best and aim to win.

Our final question to the reader: Are you a Masters racer, i.e. a woman or man in your 40s or older? If so, the recommendations in this book will most closely match what is optimal for you. If you are younger, you may also benefit from some of the ideas, but be advised that your recovery time is faster. You *can* tolerate more irregular sleep breaks well below the 4 hours recommended here, while still racing at the front. If you are over 40, beware: the greatest mistake made by Masters racers in RAAM is to take uneven or insufficient sleep breaks early on in the race, when they feel fresh, with terrible consequences later. In particular, racers often fail to sleep in the first 24 hours of the race, which is an absolute no-no that can result in depressed immune response. Pneumonia, edema, sinus infection are some of the consequences while you are riding through the desert and mountains, and dangerous fatigue ensues past the Mississippi, causing riding accidents and hallucination as the most fearsome consequences.

Of course, strong legs are still required for a good chance of winning, but in multi-day ultraendurance racing, a careful game plan based on performance physiology, and the positive mental state that comes with the right amount of rest at the right time, are more important. And that is where we can help.

The authors would like to thank Paul Carpenter for many insightful comments on the book, although all foibles of this book are the fault of the authors. We would also like to thank Sarah Young (the Honey Badger's coach) and Christine Scott for careful proofreading, as well as the RAAM crew - Lana Pohlmann, Ed Scott, Julie Turner, Roy Tylinksi, Jay Yost and Harry K. Zink – for their race information, photos, and making this book possible in the first place by crewing the Honey Badger to his win.

Martin Gruebele

Greg Scott

Urbana, IL, and San Luis Obispo, CA, August 2018

TABLE OF CONTENTS

Preface	i
Table Of Contents	v
1. What is RAAM?	1
2. The Game Plan Outlined	7
3. The 2016 race – A Quantitative Analysis	13
4. Recent RAAM Races and Alternative Strategies	31
5. Pre-race Preparation – The Racer	39
6. Pre-race Preparation – The Crew	63
7. Pre-race Preparation - Equipment and Supplies	71
8. Racer Strategy and Race Flow	83
9. Crew Schedule and Organization	101
10. Dealing with the Elements	113
11. Start and Endgame	119
12. The 2016 Race – A Chronology	127
13. Race Finance	175
14. Afterword	179
15. Bibliography	181

1. WHAT IS **RAAM**?

> *"You can't win RAAM in three days, but you certainly can lose it in three days"*
>
> Paul Carpenter, overall champion of the first Race Across the West (RAW)

The Race Across America (RAAM) runs as a single stage of about 4800 km (3000 miles), with over 51 km (170,000 feet) of elevation gain from Oceanside, California to Annapolis, Maryland. It is open to pros and amateurs alike, although most competitors are amateurs. The overall winner generally rides over 22 hours a day, and over 350 miles a day. When the weather is favorable, the fastest male racer contests RAAM in about 8 days, and the fastest Masters[1] male in about 10 days. When the weather is unfavorable, it can take the fastest male racer over 9 days, and the fastest Masters racer over 11 days. The top female racers have times comparable to the Masters male racers, and the top Masters female racers take about a day longer.

RAAM is a daunting affair, even on the scale of the most prestigious of all multi-day pro races, the Tour de France. The Tour has an elevation gain similar to RAAM, but it is usually under 2500 miles long, and contested over 23 days. The 26 mph (42 kph) on-bike speeds of the pro peloton on level ground blow away the solo RAAM winning total average speeds of 14 to 16 mph. Yet with short daily stages, plenty of time to sleep, and two rest days, the total average speed at the Tour is only 4.5 mph. Thus, it is no wonder that RAAM Executive Director Rick Boethling calls RAAM "The Toughest Cycling Race in the World." With so little rest for the racer, RAAM may be tougher on the body and mind. Jonathan Boyer, who finished 12th at the Tour, won RAAM, but he is over a day behind the RAAM course record, currently held by dedicated ultracyclist Christoph Strasser. Still, Boyer did quite well with a "sleep longer, ride faster" strategy.

Of course, single-stage races and multi-stage races of similar length are really like apples and oranges, requiring different skill sets to win. RAAM, a 3000 mile

---

[1] In this book, we use verbal designations for the RAAM age groups because many of our suggestions apply very broadly to 'Masters' racers, not just the M50-59 or F50-59 age groups. The official RAAM age groups are shown in Table 1.1 on page 3.

long time trial, is all about an individual racer balancing extreme sleep deprivation and speed, while never drafting. For yellow or green jersey contenders, the Tour is mostly about the tactics of drafting within a large peloton to save energy for decisive moments, be they sprints or climbs. Thus the difference between overall winner and second place in RAAM is often measured in many hours, whereas at the Tour it is at best a few minutes nowadays. For obvious commercial reasons (daily stages with specific towns as endpoints keeping the race together, promoting tourism, and allowing many individual 'daily wins' so many sponsors can benefit), no modern multi-day pro races will be single-stage, nor offer the winner a wooden plaque without a cash prize. To paraphrase an aphorism of climbers going up Mt. Everest, RAAM is done "because it's there."

The course of the race is very well designed. You can tell because at times, the race director is forced to re-route racers due to construction, and circumstances change for the worse: all of a sudden, there is busy traffic (like the re-route onto US 50 en route to Washington in 2016), or the road quality degrades enormously (like the re-route near Linton, Indiana, in 2016). About the only painful stretch on the regular route is US-50 in West Virginia, which is busy with truck traffic and has a litter-strewn shoulder. RAAM makes up for it with some of the most beautiful scenery in the US elsewhere along the course (Monument Valley, La Veta), or at least with straight, flat, and easily navigable roads (Kansas, Illinois). RAAM is a race after all, not a bicycle tour.

RAAM is highly demanding of the body and mind, truly pushing the limits of human physical fatigue, mental fatigue, and pain endurance.[2] In good years, about two thirds of racers finish. In hard years, only about half of the racers finish. Yet these racers all went through qualification races and are among the best ultracyclists in the world. In addition to extreme dryness (<20% humidity) and heat (often >43 °C or 110 °F) in the desert, riders also battle ice cold descents (often <5 °C or < 40 °F from Wolf Creek pass), as well as oppressive heat and humidity in the Midwest (60% humidity, 90 °F or 32 °C are not uncommon). The dangerous boredom of 800 straight, monotonous miles in the middle of the race is mentally challenging. Finally, there are infections of the lung and saddle sores, overuse injuries of the knees and back, hot feet, eye irritation, and the famous Shermer's neck, an inability to keep one's head up due to extreme muscular and nervous fatigue.

RAAM has one of the most demanding time limits of any endurance race contested by pros and amateurs together. In most shorter (and thus easier) mixed pro/amateur endurance events, amateurs are allowed at least a factor of two more time than the fastest pros. Consider the Ironman, for example: on a favorable day, the top male pro will finish in under 8 hours, but the amateurs are given about 17 hours. That's over a factor of two headroom. A marathon is run in under 2:10 by world class male athletes, under 2:25 by world class women, yet the amateurs routinely get 6 hours to complete the race, a factor of two and a half headroom. So RAAM should allow the amateur at least 16 days, if the fastest pros take 8, right? Wrong. 12 days for Open male and Masters male contestants, 12 days and 21 hours for Grandmasters and Open female is all they get. That is only a factor of one and a half overhead, a bit more for women and male 60+ racers. That cutoff alone makes RAAM one of the toughest to complete endurance events in the world. There is no 'walking the marathon' here. A DNF ("did not finish") looms at even the slightest contingency for any racer who has a time table over 11 days. This book can help racers take a quarter day off that time table, compared to conventional approaches to RAAM, or better yet – avoid a DNF.

RAAM is the brainchild of John Marino, John Howard, Michael Shermer (yes, the one with the neck problem) and Lon Haldeman, who won it the very first time as "The Great American Bicycle Race." Although RAAM once upon a time went to New York City, it has, for now, comfortably settled into its Oceanside to Annapolis route, with visits to California, Arizona, a bit of Utah, Colorado, Kansas, Missouri, a bit of Illinois, Indiana, Ohio, West Virginia, a bit of Pennsylvania, and Maryland on-and-off and at the very end.

Table 1.1 Age group designations we use in this book, and the corresponding RAAM solo categories (as of 2017).

Open male (under 50)
Masters male (50-59)
Grandmasters male (60-69 and 70+)
Open female (under 50)
Masters female (50-59)
Grandmasters female (60-69 and 70+)

The race currently comprises 55 time stations (TS) where the crew must call race headquarters and report that the racer has passed. On average, the time stations are spaced about 55 miles apart (Figure 1.1), but some are as far as 100 miles apart, and the last two are under 10 miles apart. Some of these time stations are conveniently located at Walmart stores and other shopping opportunities, have full service bicycle stores available (TS 34 in Washington).

Many are just intersections in a small town, but some are attended, such as TS 41 (Oxford) and 42 (Blanchester), whose Ohio fans, under the direction of veteran volunteer Lee Kreider, go so far as to post direction billboards along 100+ miles of route.

The terrain of RAAM is highly varied, as shown by the elevation profile in Figure 1.1. Some of the major climbing is obvious: the coastal range, Yarnell pass in Arizona and the 10,000 ft. Wolf Creek and La Veta passes. Others are less obvious on the map. The Ozarks around Camdenton is where Kansas rollers change into real climbing, and the racer knows "This ain't Kansas anymore." Brown County in Indiana offers steep climbs between Greensburg and Columbus, IN. And last, but most insidious, are the Appalachians. They look innocuous on the profile, but they offer 8 major climbs in relentless succession, with elevation gains per unit mile that outdo the Rocky Mountains. Even worse, before you get to the climbs, you get rattled on the debris-strewn shoulder of US 50 in West Virginia, while honking 18-wheelers threaten to smash your crew vehicle into you. To our racer-author at least, US 50 in West Virginia is the truly mentally tough stretch of RAAM.

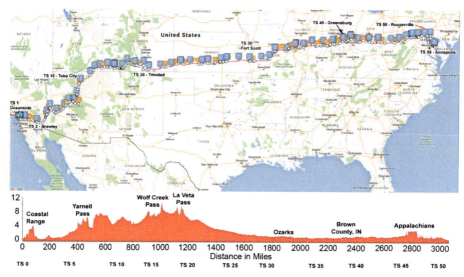

Figure 1.1 The RAAM course from Oceanside (TS 1) to Annapolis (TS 55). Time stations are shown as blue flags. Major climbing areas are indicated on the elevation profile. Elevation units: 1000s of feet (Generated with RideWithGPS using Google Maps.)

RAAM requires a crew for each racer. There are many approaches to crewing, often involving three personnel in two follow cars, a shuttle car, and RVs for sleeping. Crews of up to 10 people are not uncommon. This book advocates a much simpler approach, which we believe is more effective: Only two crew members in each of three follow vehicles, with no additional shuttling/support vehicles at all. Only a sleep/shower RV for the racer would add further utility. The total of 6 crew members can be supplemented by one more coming on board half-way through the race, as explained in Chapter 6. Each crew has its own set of specific duties that do not change from day to day. Simplicity and organization are key to the winning strategy discussed here.

During RAAM, the crew must operate in one of two modes: follow or leapfrog. In follow mode, required at nighttime (currently defined as 19:00 to 09:00 by RAAM management) and in some Indian reservations, the crew vehicle follows closely behind the racer, and is allowed a few window hand-offs each hour. Caravanning and blocking traffic are strictly prohibited, and result in time penalties. In leapfrog mode, obligatory during the day until the race reaches Kansas, the crew vehicle waits for the racer to pass, then drives ahead and parks at least 5 feet off the fog line and waits again. The stops are used to hand off water bottles to and from the racer, wave directions at confusing intersections, or buy supplies at gas stations if the racer is far enough ahead or behind. From Kansas on, crews may use either mode during the day. The approach explained in this book will largely involve night riding, and thus largely follow mode.

One thing that has become easier over the years is tracking the competition. The race in 2016 used a satellite GPS unit the size of your thumb. It slips in the racer's back pocket and lasts for essentially the whole race, although management recommends replacing the battery when you cross the Mississippi. Your crew can track every racer, their sleep breaks, and strategy, and some of this data is discussed in Chapter 3. This is a good place to mention that The Honey Badger strictly instructed his crew not to tell him about standings for the first 7 days. You must race your own race early on, and resist any temptation to ride longer, faster, or sleep less just because another racer in your category is ahead of you by 100 miles. If they are stronger, you can do nothing about it, and if they are not, you will just be drawn into the same fate that they will suffer by Day 8 of the race, jeopardizing your placement at the finish.

Speaking of tracking, one of the most important items that RAAM management will supply to you are three route books. These contain marginally useful grayscale maps, but very helpful cue sheets from one TS to the next. It is fair to say that the route book is as integral an element of RAAM as the racer and the crew, and "resetting the odometer" is a task that should become second nature to the crew when reporting the racer's passage at each TS. The details of good route book usage are discussed in Chapter 8. The route book is absolutely critical even when the racer and crew have independent GPS.

RAAM is an undertaking expensive both in terms of time, as well as funds. As discussed in Chapter 5, three years were necessary to prepare the Honey Badger, and as discussed in Chapter 13, over $20,000 were spent, excluding bicycles. Many European teams are quasi-professional and heavily sponsored, with bills upwards of $80,000. Their professional approach - relying on highly trained crews, not conscripted family members, on rental vehicles, not uncle's rusty van, and on data-driven performance, not gut feeling - often pays off in terms of podium performances. In the Open male category (25-49), the US has not won in well over a decade. In the male Masters category (50-59), things are a bit more relaxed when it comes to no-expenses-spared, and American solo riders have fared better against the European racers. For a US solo rider who is not prepared to spend $80,000 on RAAM, the 50+ competition offers a much better statistical chance at the famous wooden USA plaque that goes to the winner in each category. Money is time, though. For example, we estimate (see Chapter 11) that we could have finished about 4 hours faster by spending another $6,000 on an RV with a shower, bed, and RV crew.

RAAM has many sister races that can serve as qualifiers and practice races, for RAAM solo is not a walk-on race. RAAM qualification currently remains active for 3 years, and we recommend getting qualified early in the training cycle, at least 2 years out from RAAM itself. This book recommends a special approach to two-person team RAAM for qualification and training (if you have a friend willing to suffer with you, see Chapter 5). In addition, the Race Across the West (RAW), RAAM Challenges, and other long distance races such as the Heart of the South, Tortour, the 508, or even long randonnées such as Paris – Brest – Paris (the author's favorite) are also excellent practice, even if not all can serve as qualifiers. Finally, many 200-mile or 12-hour races, including Ironman triathlons, offer excellent endurance practice. We encourage staying away from 24-hour cycling races because we believe they are counterproductive during training, as discussed in Chapter 5.

Despite its great challenges, RAAM does not have to grind the racer down. The Honey Badger is seen smiling in every race photo because he followed the strategy of long daytime sleep shifts and long uninterrupted night cycling shifts that we advocate for the Masters racer with a strong circadian rhythm. We discuss the outline of this strategy in the next chapter.

2. THE GAME PLAN OUTLINED

The approach advocated in this book is predicated on two general premises:

1. A strong Masters racer can ride at about the same on-bike speed as the Open podium winners, by resting regularly once each day for an optimum number of hours.[3,4]

2. It is imperative that the hottest hours of the day, generally noon to 16:00, be avoided in favor of night riding. The dehydration and heat stress during the mid-day hours take the greatest toll on the racer.[5]

Point number 1 above may seem audacious, but we will see based on the numbers crunched post-race for RAAM 2016 (Chapter 3) that it is quite possible. It is worth mentioning here that point 1 does not require pro-level athletic gifts. The Honey Badger has a functional threshold power of 280 W (defined here as the sustained power in a flat time trial for 1 hour). That power output is sufficient for a 58-minute, 40 kilometer time trial; a climbing power of 4.5 W/kg; and a VAM of 1000 m/h.[†] These are solid numbers, but by no means close to international elite level (more like 400 W, 6 W/kg and 1600 m/h). Many strong Masters ultracyclists can boast numbers like the Honey Badger's, and they could ride similar average speeds on the bike as the Open racers on the overall podium, just like the Honey Badger did. The improved physical and mental state that comes with executing our race plan of regular day sleep and night riding is at least as important as sheer cycling strength.

Point number 2 should be self-explanatory. Daytime riding in the Arizona desert at 110 °F, or in the 90 °F Kansas humidity, really takes it out of the racer. Nighttime temperatures during the race generally vary between the high 70s in the plains, to 40s in Rocky Mountain passes. Such temperatures can be dealt with easily by using appropriate clothing, minimizing excessive dehydration and symptoms of dryness such as chapped lips or red eyes.

Once these two points are accepted, the 5 **keystones** of a winning Masters race strategy follow almost automatically:

1. The Masters racer should **sleep approximately 4 hours each day**.

[†] VAM, or 'mean ascent velocity,' is the maximum vertical meters a cyclist can climb in an hour, usually in units of meters per hour. It is the climbing analog of functional threshold power in flat time trials.

2. The Masters racer should **sleep during the middle of the day**, typically 12:00-16:00 local time, and ride at night, to avoid the hottest parts of the day. The mid-day start of the race is an exception, as may be the last day of the race.

3. The Masters racer **should ride regularly between rest breaks**, essentially non-stop except for short crew exchanges.

4. The daily **crew exchanges should be stationary**. One takes place during the racer's sleep break, and the other two will fall in the nighttime. The stationary exchanges are utilized for careful hygiene breaks, which minimize the other pitfall besides exhaustion: many racers quit because of entirely preventable saddle sores and infections.

5. The optimal crew distribution to execute this plan consists of **three follow vehicles with two crew members in each vehicle**. The three crews split the racer's on-bike hours evenly into 6-7 hour shifts. No shuttle vehicles are required, although an RV for the racer is optional if the race budget permits it.

Let us analyze each of these keystones, which were implemented by the Honey Badger during the 2016 RAAM race, in a little more detail.

Keystone 1 is a direct consequence of point 1: A Master racer simply cannot regenerate in an hour a day off the bike, as some young racers like Christoph Strasser can. If you have a strong circadian rhythm, and you need to go to bed around the same time each day in order to fall asleep, short breaks at random times simply will not work.[6] As a default, 50- to 60-year-olds will require about 4 hours of sleep (roughly 2 typical REM cycles[†]) during each race day in order to be able to maintain a heart rate around HR_{race} = 160-age, or in the 100-110 beat per minute range during the race. This number, of course, differs somewhat from person to person, and is discussed more in Chapter 5, "Pre-race preparation: the racer." However, it is very unlikely that the optimal sleep duration will fall outside the range of 3 to 5 hours for you. Any less sleep, and sometime between days 6 and 8 you will notice drastic performance

---

[†] REM = 'rapid eye movement' refers to the final phase of sleep in a typical *ca.* 90-120 minute long deep-light-REM sleep cycle. REM sleep is often accompanied by dreaming, high brain activity, and muscle atonia (to protect the sleeper from moving in his or her dreams). The whole sleep cycle (not just the REM part) is important for recovery, but it is easiest to wake up at the end of REM sleep, when sleep is lightest, rather than waking up in the middle of deep sleep. Our crew used this knowledge to optimize racer wake-up.

deterioration: low heart rate, excessive sensitivity to the heat of the day, nodding off on the bike, and irritability or confusion. Any more sleep, and you are wasting time in bed: you'll feel fresher of course, but the extra hours slept no longer translate into equal hours gained racing. Let's face it, the racers must race in misery during RAAM, especially during its latter stages, or they are not getting all they can out of themselves. But overdo the misery early on, and racers will fail to reach their best overall performance. Do not race RAAM like a three-day race.

The 4-hour sleep block has two other major advantages for many Masters racers: improved nutritional intake and immune system performance.[7] As you age, your liver's and intestines' ability to process food and keep up glycogen storage declines. Very short sleep breaks deprive your digestive system of an extended period of blood flow, needed for complete processing of food intake and maximum glycogen storage. As a result, you become 'irregular' during a multi-day effort, and your appetite cannot keep up with your body's glycogen deprivation. This can make you hit a wall after 3 to 4 days. By sleeping a full 4-hour block every day from the outset, your system can actually digest real food, and keep glycogen levels adequate to make it through a 10+ day race without riding 'bonked'. In addition, your immune system remains functional longer, staving off race-ending infections or edema. Immune suppression will happen to you even if 'you don't feel tired and could go on.' It's like the old adage about hydration: when you feel very thirsty on the bike, it is too late to drink; when you feel very fatigued on the bike, it IS too late to sleep.

Keystone 2 follows directly from point 2: The afternoon hours are very hard in the Arizona Desert heat, in the brutal UV exposure of the Rocky Mountain sunlight, or in the oppressive humidity of the Midwestern US.[5] The path to success is to simply get rid of 4 to 5 of these hours altogether (assuming you sleep for about 4 hours and shower/eat/prep for another 0.5 hours), and to split the remainder into two short, manageable segments. The Honey Badger typically went to bed around noon, got up around 16:00 local time, rode in the heat for 3-4 hours before the temperature dropped to more benign nighttime values. Then, after a comfortable night and early morning ride, he only had to tackle 3-4 hot hours again before the next noon rest stop. Splitting the heat into two short 60-mile segments makes it absolutely tolerable. It energized our racer for the rest of the ride, and is key to maintaining an on-bike speed comparable to the pros.

"But how can I go to sleep at noon?" you ask, skeptically. It's simple: artificial jetlag. The Honey Badger gradually jetlagged himself two weeks prior to the race to go to bed at 04:00 PDT (Pacific daylight savings time) and wake up at 11:00. Leaving lights on at night and darkening the room during the day helped.[8] This made it easy to be ready for the race start at about 1 PM on Tuesday, ride through the first moderate afternoon in California and through the night, and then go to bed dead-tired around 10:00 at Sheffler's motel in Salome AZ after a 342-mile ride on the first day. From then on, a single 10:00-14:00 ... 11:00-15:00 ... 12:00-16:00 PM ... 13:00-17:00 rest break, followed by riding approximately 300 miles/day, is maintained with few exceptions, while the racer and crew progress towards the East Coast and go to bed a little later each day.

Note that several racers in 2017 and 2018 used this strategy successfully. Others also tried, but could not keep up the mid-day sleep schedule after a couple of days. This may be due to insufficient jet-lagging before the race to prepare for the unusual sleep times. A compromise (see Chapter 4) that worked well for some racers is to split the sleep into a regular daytime rest and nighttime rest, while still keeping a very regular riding schedule of about 10 to 11 hours on the bike in-between. This may also help racers who have a tough time staying in the saddle for 19-20 hours each day.

Keystone 3 follows from point 2 and **keystone 2**: If you are sleeping in a motel or RV for 4 hours during the day, you have to be riding the rest of the time. No idle breaks are allowed, only two 10-minute stationary crew exchanges (see Chapter 9), weather breaks, or contingencies such as flat tires. The Honey Badger rode 18 to 22 hours a day between his sleep breaks, depending on the location of motel stops. Even more ideal is a very even schedule, which would be made possible by an RV that meets the racer around noon each day for the sleep break. Riding about 20 hours a day is not as daunting as it seems, although it requires careful preparation in terms of mental conditioning, entertainment during the ride, and most importantly, racer hygiene and saddle choice to avoid sores (see Chapters 5 and 8).

Keystone 4 follows automatically from the schedule enforced by mid-day sleeping. As discussed in detail in later logistical chapters, one crew will pick up the racer at the end of his or her sleep in the late afternoon. A second crew accompanies the racer from late night until the early morning hours. A third and final will drop the racer off to sleep around noon, and leave. Three crews splitting the evening, night and morning shifts will invariably exchange during RAAM night time, which is defined as 19:00 to 09:00 in the newest rules from 2016 onwards.

While stationary team exchanges may seem disadvantageously slow, the Honey Badger used them to his advantage: while the crews swapped bikes, crates, bottles, batteries and other items, the racer performed kit changes and hygiene—which took about 10 minutes—during each crew exchange and at the motel. In addition, the brief but regular stops permit blood flow in the seating area, indispensable to keeping the racer in the saddle unfazed for long hours. One of the most insidious problems during RAAM is infections in the seating area, such as saddle sores. Following a simple procedure, the Honey Badger never got any, although sitting in a saddle for over 19 hours a day for 10 or 11 days will still make you very, very sore. But more about that in Chapter 8.

Keystone 5 of our winning strategy - last but not least - is to make the race enjoyable, but very busy, for the crew. Every racer should remember that his or her crewmates are giving away almost 3 weeks of their lives, typically from June 10 to June 28, not counting crew preparation outside of the race window. Yes, they may be good friends and family members, or maybe even hired hands, but they will work with the racer much better if they can sleep a reasonable amount on a regular schedule, do not have to drive behind the racer at snail's pace for more than 7 hours each day, and have a little time for sightseeing along the route, or even just for doing their shopping for the racer unhurried. The three follow vehicle strategy also works well if contingencies arise: car accidents, weather that prevents a crew from making a rendezvous, or a crew just plain oversleeping. All these things happened to the Honey Badger in 2016, but he never noticed them because the three crews were able to smooth all the ruffles. Why only two crew members per vehicle? To keep the peace! The psychological reasons for this will be discussed in Chapter 6, but let it be said now that the night crew (called Crew #2 later in the book) could benefit from a third member late in the race, and so it was implemented. Furthermore, an RV crew is needed if the racer chooses mobile sleeping over the motel approach. The RV undoubtedly could have saved the Honey Badger several hours of race time over the motels, and is worth considering if you have the financial means.

The game plan outlined above is a calculated risk, like all good racing. Following it, you will very likely lag behind other Masters riders for the first 6 days, and catch up only when they get tired while you remain relatively fresh. There are of course many details that make the overall game plan work, but it is straightforward: the racer sleeps about 4 hours mid-day starting at the end of the very first riding shift,[9] rides throughout the night, has three crews of two people tending him or her for about 7 hours each, and makes use of stationary exchanges for hygiene to keep the most precious part of the racer, the saddle contact surface, functional from start to finish. The legs of a well-trained racer (riding 1000 to 2000 miles/month in the years leading up to the race) can handle RAAM without a problem. That leaves only the racer's mind as a weak link – however, good entertainment and a crew chief who sticks to the plan will help with that.

3. THE 2016 RACE – A QUANTITATIVE ANALYSIS

A race as long as RAAM, and with as much history as RAAM, provides a wealth of data to examine. There are many quantitative resources available online, for example segments of the race posted as "Events" on RideWithGPS, the software we used to plan the race and store Martin's race information. The official GPS tracking of the race was contracted by RAAM management to Trackleaders.com. Much useful information about the race is publicly available there. Keith Wolcott has a number of quantitative tools available at http://www.teamwolcottcycling.com.

In this chapter, we put the 2016 race performances in context with the race's history. We dig into the details of the GPS tracking data to identify successful racing strategies, and examine performance data for the 2016 Masters winner in light of our strategy of "Regular rest during the day – ride all night," and the **five keystones** that derive from it:

1. The Master racer sleeps about 4 hours per day.
2. The racer jet-lags to sleep in the middle of the day, when it is hottest.
3. Race uninterrupted for 19-21 hours through the night until late morning.
4. Make use of stationary crew exchanges for racer hygiene breaks.
5. Two crew members in three vehicles keeps the crew busy yet rested with three 6-7 hour shifts.

The last two keystones will be examined in detail in Chapters 6, 9 and 12, which focus on the crew. A more global data analysis of recent RAAM races, on the new ~3070 mile course through Camp Verde, is presented in Chapter 4.

Our conclusions based on the data can be summarized as follows: Masters winners can ride as fast on-bike as racers on the Open podium, but need more rest to achieve that on-bike speed. A regular sleep pattern is optimal for good race performance. Sleep duration is a compromise between performance deterioration due to insufficient sleep and slow progress due to too much sleep; around 4 hours is optimal for Masters racers. Riding during cool hours of the night yields better overall performance than riding during the hot day. Racer strength and strategy are more important than external influences (e.g. weather) in determining race finish time (70% *vs.* 30%). Our racer had an average Masters winning time when compared to other years. In such a case, optimum strategy becomes particularly important, as the racer cannot simply "ride away from the field." Finally, it is possible to recover from a lack-of-sleep error, but the consequences last for several days. Accumulation of sleep errors is probably the major factor in race performance. All of these conclusions reinforce the first 3 **keystones**.

The 2016 Race in Context

RAAM has been contested annually since 1982, which provides a large set of historical data. Here, we limit our statistical analysis to the years 2000-2016. For over half of these years, beginning in 2008, RAAM was completed on the Oceanside to Annapolis route. The race includes some variation in course and distance. RAAM 2016 was one of the longer rides at 3089 miles, RAAM 2013 was one of the shorter ones at 2997 miles. We do *not* take these few percent variations into account by scaling finish times or other data accordingly. While RAAM has grown to include several categories with options for different riding equipment such as recumbents, this analysis is also limited only to those solo riders completing the race on standard equipment.

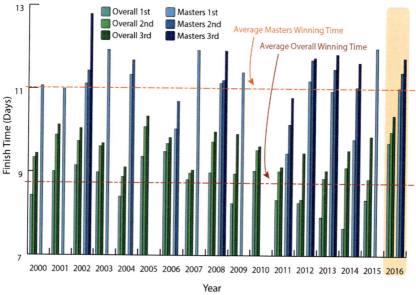

Figure 3.1. Finish times for top three overall male solo riders and top three male Masters solo riders since 2000. In 2005 and 2010, there were no Masters solo finishers on standard equipment and there are other years where there were not enough Masters finishers to fill the podium. Note that Masters is defined in this figure as the 50-59 age group, though there were several years where finishers from the 60-69 age group would have filled empty spots. For example, in 2008 David Jones finished ahead of several 50-59 age group finishers and would be in 2nd place on this graph (267.4 hours).

Figure 3.1 shows the top three times in the 18-49 and 50-59 categories from 2000 to 2016. The finish time for the overall RAAM winner from 2000-2016 has ranged from Christoph Strasser's record of 7 days 15 hours 56 min (7:15:56) to 9:17:09 with an average of 8.72 ± 0.14 days. The Masters winning times have ranged from 9:11:02 to 11:23:33 with an average of 11.03 ± 0.19 days. On average, the overall winner has beaten the top Masters rider to the East Coast by 2.3 days.

The full range of winning times, about 48 hours, is large for both the Open and Masters categories. The route is long, thus many variables that can affect performance have ample time to affect each racer. These variables include race distance, weather, rider strength and race strategy. We will make the argument that external factors such as weather and distance, although they affect everyone's time, cannot account for the range of winning times. Rather, as we will argue below, race strategy is an important factor.

One way to consider race difficulty is to look at the distribution of finishing times in various race categories. Figure 3.2 shows the distributions of winning times since 2000. 2016 was the slowest overall male finish in the study window, and nearly the slowest overall female finish. These results, like the 52% DNF rate in 2016, suggest a challenging year.

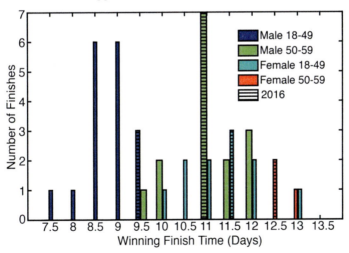

Figure 3.2. Histogram of winning times since 2000. The very fastest Masters winning times (green) are comparable to the slowest Male Open winning times (purple).

Still, is overall race difficulty the main factor? If a race is difficult due to conditions experienced by all racers (e.g. weather), we expect the performances of different racers to be strongly correlated: Open male racers will be faster than Masters male or Open female racers, but all will be slower together in a difficult year. Let us examine two such correlations.

First, we quantify the difficulty of a given year by looking at the percent of solo racers who do not finish the race. From 2000-2016, the DNF percentage has ranged from as low as 27% to as high as 58% with an average of 41 ± 3%. 2016 saw the slowest overall winning time, and one of only four DNF rates exceeding 50% since 2000. We surmise that headwinds and crosswinds in the central US affected the solo riders (up to 15 mph SE winds in eastern Colorado and Kansas), while hot weather in the West (up to 120 °F at Blythe) affected the teams.

Nonetheless, we find that there is only a weak correlation between the overall finishing time and the DNF rate, or the Masters winner and the Open winner finish time (Figure 3.3). The expected trend does exist, but it is small. Factors besides race conditions must play a role.

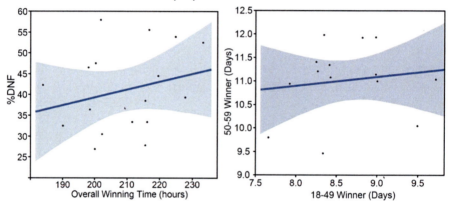

Figure 3.3. The DNF rate and Open winner's finishing time (left), as well as the Masters winner and Open winner's finishing time (right) are only weakly correlated. Thus effects other than global ones (course length, hot year, etc.) must dominate race performance.

External challenges such as a hot year or a harder course cannot be the whole story. One anecdotal piece of evidence is that in 2016, the Honey Badger won the Masters category with a time almost exactly the average of the winning Masters finish times since 2000. Yet he ended up only 1.3 days behind the male overall winner, rather than the average of 2.3 days. This discrepancy suggests that racer strength and race strategy can be as important as weather or distance, factors that affect all racers nearly equally.

Figure 3.4 shows a stronger trend to support the anecdotal evidence in favor of an optimal race strategy: When the overall winner is slower, the Masters winner is closer to the overall winner. This is despite the similar range of times (about 2 days) for the two categories shown in Figure 3.2.

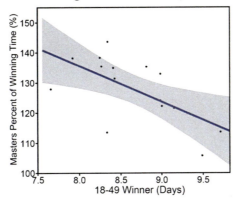

Figure 3.4. Correlation of Masters winning time as a percent of overall winning time with the overall winning time. When the overall winner is slower, the Masters winner tends to finish closer to the overall leader.

Figure 3.5A shows the same information as Figure 3.2, but focuses on the male Overall and Masters categories. While the 2016 Masters winning time was average among Masters winning finish times, it was fast compared to the Male Open winning time. One way to normalize for the effects of the variations in difficulty across the years is to look at the Masters winning time as a percentage of the overall winning time. Figure 3.5B shows the distribution of these percentages since 2000. In 2016, the Masters winner rode 114% of the overall winner's time, the third best performance on this metric since 2000.

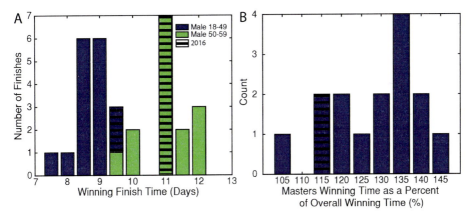

Figure 3.5. A. Histogram of winning times for 18-49 (blue) and 50-59 (green) age categories since 2000. B. Histogram of the masters winning time relative to the overall winning time (i.e. Overall/Masters x 100%). The patterned bars represent the bins containing the 2016 race.

To summarize this section, external factors do play a role in winning time differences from year to year (we estimate *ca.* 30%), but racer strength and strategy are probably more important (we estimate *ca.* 70%). In the next section of this chapter, we will argue that it is most likely race strategy, not unusual strength that contributes most of the difference. This is good news for the Masters racer with the right strategy.

Tracking Data and Rest Analysis

An analysis of the riding and rest patterns for the racers in 2016 is useful for validating the strategy outlined in this book. The 2016 edition of RAAM introduced the use of a long battery life GPS tracker that utilized satellite communication, rather than cellular communication for reporting back data. This provided an unprecedented wealth of data for the event that allowed crews and fans to monitor the riding and resting behavior of the racing field in real-time.

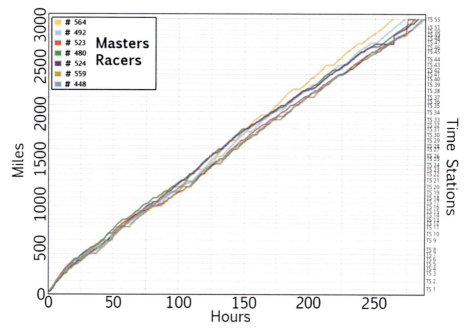

Figure 3.6. Race distance for Masters riders in 2016 as a function of race time. The Masters winner did not take the race lead until the last third of the race, likely due to better rest in the early stages of the race. The second place Masters finisher, who had a fairly consistent sleep schedule (though less of it, and at night), also did not emerge in second place until late in the race. Figure modified from the RAAM live tracking website.

This section explores the rest patterns for the 2016 RAAM, focusing on the Masters riders. In short, the data suggest that the most successful Masters riders utilized uninterrupted ride cycles and relatively long rest cycles at very regular time intervals, with the rests taken during the middle of the day correlating best with fast race performance. This is supported by the physiology literature.[3] Figure 3.6 shows an overview of racer progress in the 2016 Masters race. The most consistently rested rider was buried at the back of the field at the beginning of the race. Then, skipping sleep was advantageous to the other racers. However, the most consistently rested racer emerged as the leader in the second half of the race. Later, not skipping sleep early on was a major factor his win, as the analysis below shows.

The simplest approach to examining sleep schedules is by inspection of speed *vs.* time graphs. Figure 3.7 shows the speed *vs.* time traces for a selection of racers from 2016. The Masters winner is shown at the top. He rode long on-bike shifts averaging over 19 hours, punctuated by daytime rest periods off the bike averaging over 4 hours. The rest periods all took place at nearly the same time of day each day. When the rider's sleep schedule shifted too late at the end of Day 4 and performance declined due to lack of sleep, the crew shortened the rider's next day of riding to restore sleeping during the hot middle of the day. Only during the last rest period on Day 10 was there any deviation from the rest pattern, once finishing was a near inevitability. Most importantly, the Honey Badger started the regular schedule on day 1.

When the same traces are examined for other racers, the features that were prominent in the Masters winner's trace are not readily apparent. The second and third place Masters riders also showed regular sleep habits, but their sleep was shorter, took place largely during nighttime hours, and they skipped rest on day 1. Thus insufficient sleep, and riding in the heat of the day are possible reasons for slower performance. The 6th place Masters rider added in very short rests during the day but still slept mostly at night. The Masters female winner began to rest more during the day in the second half of the race, and her performance improved. Also shown for comparison are some younger Male Open riders, both male and female, who can clearly tolerate irregular short rests, while still riding at high speeds. That is not to say that more regular rests during the day might not have improved their performance. As discussed earlier, the Masters winner was only 1.3 days behind the Male Open winner, rather than the average of 2.3 days observed over 16 years of RAAM racing. It is possible that even the Male Open winner could have benefited from moving his short sleep breaks to take place during the day only.

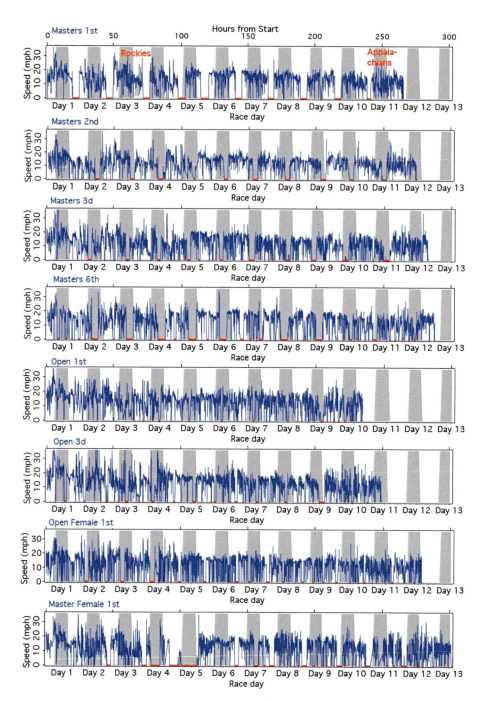

Figure 3.7. Speed traces (blue) for a representative sample of RAAM 2016 racers. Night hours are indicated by the gray boxes. The rest blocks, where the speed was 0 mph, are highlighted in red. Only the Masters winner put in a long sleep break in the first 24 hours.

An important feature in Figure 3.7 that distinguishes the Masters winner from the rest of the field is that he started regular rest on Day 1. There was no period with more than 24 hours of riding at the start.[9] RAAM is not a 24-hour race, and the regular schedule should be kept from Day 1. Further evidence for this is provided at the end of this chapter, where we discuss what happened when our racer missed a single regular sleep period.

Figure 3.8 compresses the traces from Figure 3.8 down to a simple bar graph, showing the total amount of time each rider was moving *vs.* the time stopped. As highlighted by the blue dashed line, four of the top five overall riders rode approximately the same speed when on the bike, 14.7 ± 0.2 mph. And so did the Masters winner! This result suggests that in a race of this length, the most successful Masters racers will rest just enough to maintain the same on-bike speed as the Male Open winner. The remaining Masters either slept too much (5th place) or rode too much (2nd, 3d and 6th place), trading a day of sleep for a day of riding without any overall gain. The Open male 4th place racer, in contrast, overslept, and was unable to make up for it with his faster on-bike speed.

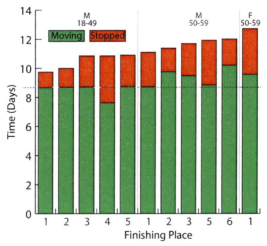

Figure 3.8. Total moving and stopped times for top racers in 2016. (4th place Masters had a GPS problem and is excluded from the data.) The dotted blue line is a guide to the eye to highlight that most of the top open riders and the Masters winner rode approximately the same speed on the bike. Most of the other Masters riders spent too much time riding and too little sleeping, while one open and one Masters rider spent too much time sleeping.

Our Masters winner posted an average winning time among the 2000-2016 winning times (Figure 3.5). We believe that the strongest Masters riders in the world, who can go over a day faster (middle of Figure 3.6A), will still benefit from our strategy. They may be able to average the same on-bike speed as the strongest Male Open riders (above 16 mph on the bike), but we suggest that they would not be able to do it without regular sleep breaks during the day.

Table 3.1. Rest variables for top Open and Masters racers in 2016. T is the total race time in hours, and the other variables are explained in the text below. The largest values of Z, R, and D in each category with more than 1 rider are in bold.

Racer position	T	L	L/T	Z	R	D
Masters 1st	264.8	55.8	21%	**3.0**	**3.8**	**78%**
Masters 2nd	273.8	42.9	16%	2.6	2.8	18%
Masters 3rd	282.0	58.9	21%	1.7	1.3	32%
Masters 4th *	284.4	63.9	23%	0.8	1.7	51%
Masters 5th	287.5	85.1	30%	1.2	2.0	43%
Masters 6th	288.0	52.6	18%	1.7	1.7	33%
Overall 1st	233.2	28.0	12%	2.1	1.3	44%
Overall 2nd **	239.5	45.3	19%	0.9	1.7	16%
Overall 3rd	248.9	44.2	18%	2.1	1.7	50%
Overall 4th	258.3	76.9	30%	1.3	1.1	43%
Overall 5th	261.7	58.2	22%	**2.3**	**2.1**	**63%**
Female 1st	278.4	60.9	22%	1.9	1.6	54%
Masters Female 1st	301.4	81.7	27%	1.0	0.9	59%

* The Masters 4th place had a GPS problem; values are excluded from Fig. 3.10.
** Overall 2nd place spent several hours in the hospital. The involuntary stop overestimates sleep duration and underestimates regularity, so the data are excluded from Fig. 3.10.

We now introduce five variables to quantify the patterns that emerge from Figure 3.7. Table 3.1 shows these five variables for the top Masters and Open racers. T is the total race time in hours. The five variables are as follows:

1. L is the total rest time in hours. Rest periods are defined as breaks >0.5 hours at under 2 mph. Thus very short breaks are not captured by L.

2. L/T is the fraction of race time spent resting. Too much rest slows down the racer because of time wasted, too little rest because of slower riding.

3. Z measures the consistency of the length of the rests. Values above 2 are highly consistent, values from 1.4 to 2 are fairly consistent, values 1.3 to 1 are fairly inconsistent, and values below 1 are highly inconsistent rest durations.

4. R measures the regularity of the length of the ride segments. Values above 2 are highly consistent ride lengths, values from 1.4 to 2 are fairly consistent, values 1.3 to 1 are fairly inconsistent, and values below 1 are highly inconsistent ride lengths.

5. D is the fraction of the rest taken during daytime hours; the larger D, the more time a racer spent sleeping during the day instead of at night.

Z is defined as

$$Z = \frac{\bar{z}}{\sigma_z},$$

where $\bar{z}$ is the average length of rest breaks and σ_z is the standard deviation[†] of the length of the rest breaks. For the purposes of computing Z, rests were counted only when they exceeded 30 minutes, as a proxy for identifying sleep periods; rests shorter than 30 minutes were lumped into the riding times between breaks.

R is defined by the equation

$$R = \frac{\bar{r}}{\sigma_r},$$

where $\bar{r}$ is the average riding time between rest breaks and σ_r is the standard deviation of the riding time between breaks. The bigger the value of variables Z and R, the more consistent the length of the rest breaks and riding times.

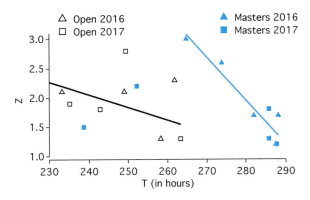

Figure 3.9. Correlation of more regular rest (Z), with shorter total race time (T). The riders depicted here are the male riders in Tables 3.1 and 3.2. The lines are least squares fits to the Open and Masters data. Improvement is steeper for Masters riders, but noticeable even for the Open riders. Note that the two youngest Masters riders of 2017 (50 & 51 years of age) defied the correlation, riding races as fast as the Open riders with comparable Z values. Clearly, some individuals can tolerate shorter and less regular sleep even at age 50.

[†] For readers not familiar with the "standard deviation": it measures how much a quantity varies about the average. For example, a racer who sometimes sleeps 30 minutes, sometimes 6 hours, will have a large standard deviation. A racer who always sleeps exactly 4 hours has a standard deviation of zero. Thus, as the variable Z becomes larger, the more regular the length of the sleep break. As the variable R becomes larger, the more regular the ride length.

Ultimately, the fastest riders tend to spend the smallest possible fraction of their total race time resting. Overall 1st rested only 28 hours in Table 3.1. There comes a trade-off, however, when the rest is insufficient, causing on-bike speed to decrease and the total race time to increase. The strategy outlined in this book can be stated mathematically: Our Masters winner had the right value of L (4 hours/day, excluding shower and breakfast) and the largest values of Z, R, and D of any racer: very regular rest periods (large Z), very regular on-bike shifts (large R), and resting mostly during the day, not at night (large D). By averaging 2 cycles of sleep (deep-light-REM) per shift at the same time each day, the Honey Badger rode about the same on-bike speed as the overall winner, and spent less time on the bike than the other Masters racers.

The value of the regularity of rest is highlighted in Figure 3.9. The Masters riders show a strong trend toward better race performance when the individual rest periods are regular, as indicated by a high value of Z for shorter T. The same trend exists for Open racers, but not as strongly: younger racers are more tolerant of irregular sleep.

High Z means regular sleep, not large quantity of sleep: our Masters rider has neither the shortest, nor the longest value of L in Table 3.1. His total rest (55 hours) is right in the middle. Too long a sleep does not help: 5th place in Table 3.1 averaged much more stopped time than 1st place, far more than 4 hours per day. The 4th place Open male racer also slept too much (Figure 3.9). The right amount of very regular sleep is what works.

Have a look at Table 3.1 again: Master #2 rode regularly and rested regularly, but had too little rest (L = 43 hours instead of 55 hours rest), and did not rest during the day (D = 18% instead of 78% daytime sleep). Master #3 rode and slept too irregularly, and did too much riding during the day (D = 32% is better than 18%, but still well below 78%).

Table 3.1 reveals the optimum sleep amount for Masters *vs.* Male Open racers. About 20% is optimal for Masters (3d place Open is approaching Masters age). A Male overall win requires 6 to 12% - (see also Chapter 4). Masters who sleep under 16% or over 22% are getting too fatigued or sleeping too much for an optimal performance.

Another way to visualize the different resting strategies of racers is to look at the accumulated rest for sets of the riders throughout the course of the race. Figure 3.10 shows the rest accumulated by the Masters riders who finished the 2016 RAAM. The 3rd place overall finisher, who was not a Masters rider is shown for comparison. The regular pattern of long riding and resting cycles already discussed for the Masters winner is readily apparent in this representation as well: the blue curve looks like a staircase. There were three emergent patterns among the other racers that are highlighted in the Figure and discussed in the following paragraphs: resting less throughout the race; resting too little early in the race, followed by excessive rest later in the race; and resting more in total but with a less regular pattern.

Pattern 1: Resting less throughout the race. Many Masters racers chose to rest less throughout the race than the Masters winner. They are highlighted in orange in Figure 3.10. Other than the Masters winner, only the second place rider in the Masters category showed a riding/resting pattern with a high level of regularity. It is unsurprising that the second spot on the podium went to another rider using a consistent schedule. However, three features distinguish this racer from the winner. One is that he slept largely during the cooler night hours, continuing to ride through the heat of the day. The second is that the total accumulated rest during the race was too close to the younger racers who can recover more quickly. Finally, he skipped sleep on day 1. As shown in Figure 3.10, the second place Masters racer accumulated less rest than a younger rider who was 3rd overall in the race. There were several other Masters racers, also highlighted in orange, who slept comparable amounts to the third place overall racer and finished further down the ranks. The third place overall racer is approaching Masters age in 2016, but he has been one of the most consistent top performers in the history of RAAM. There are likely few Masters riders who can match his on-bike speeds while resting as little as he does, although he was beaten to 1st place Master by a few hours in 2017.

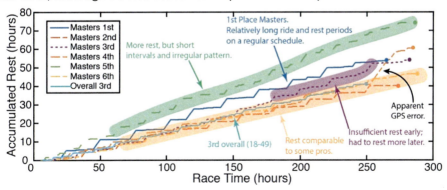

Figure 3.10. Accumulated rest for Masters finishers for RAAM 2016. The 3rd overall finisher in the 18-49 category is also included as a solid light blue line for comparison.

Pattern 2: Lack of sufficient rest early in the race, followed by additional rest later in the race. This is highlighted in purple in Figure 3.10. This racer ultimately rested more than the Masters winner, but was unable to maintain the same on-bike performance. It is likely that this rider would have benefited from more rest earlier in the race and less later in the race, thus leveling out the riding and resting efforts. It is the same idea as in any time trial: go evenly so there is plenty in the tank for the second half of the race.

Pattern 3: Accumulation of a lot of irregular rest.[6] This is highlighted in green in Figure 3.11. Additional rest likely benefited this rider on the bike, but the resting sequences were more frequent and highly irregular, with large variations in both riding and resting times, and again without the benefit of regular sleep during daylight hours. Ultimately, there is a balance between additional sleep benefitting the rider on the bike and the time lost while sitting motionless. The data suggest that this middle ground is best achieved with a highly regular riding/resting pattern including *ca.* 4 hours of sleep during the day, no more. Wake-up should occur during the REM or light sleep phase.

It is also informative to carry out the same accumulated rest analysis for the riders who did not finish RAAM 2016. Figure 3.11 shows the accumulated rest for the Masters riders who did not finish, along with the Masters winner and the overall 3rd place rider for comparison. The same three patterns emerge as were apparent for the slower Masters finishers, and are highlighted with the same color scheme used in Figure 3.10. Without exception, the riders who did not finish lacked a regular pattern in their riding/resting sequences.

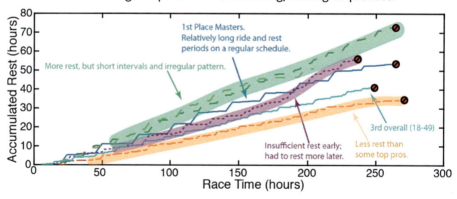

Figure 3.11. Accumulated rest for racers who did not finish RAAM 2016. The Masters winner and the 3rd place overall rider are included as solid lines for comparison.

Our rest analysis leads to several pieces of guidance for the future Masters RAAM racer who wants to maximize his or her chances of winning. An optimal approach to riding well is a regular sleep schedule with sufficiently long rests built in. The more erratic the schedule, the more exhausted the rider becomes over the course of the race. Even when regular, the sleep must be sufficient. The Masters winner aimed for roughly 4 hours during rest periods to be able to maintain optimal performance on the bike. Most Masters riders likely cannot maintain a high level of on-bike performance with substantially less sleep than this. Finally, establishing sleep schedules to sleep during the hottest—and often windiest—hours of the day maximizes riding performance during more favorable night riding conditions. Train at night, and the night will be your friend.

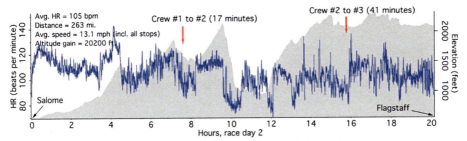

Figure 3.12 Heart rate for a relatively good day of riding (2nd shift). The crew exchanges were still relatively slow (>10 minutes), due to racer and crew inexperience under real-life conditions.

Performance Data

Up to this point, the comparisons of resting and riding strategies have been comparisons between riders. The value of good rest, however, can be validated by examining specific biometric data from a single rider. Here we briefly discuss the heart rate and power data for the 2016 Masters winner. While the Masters winner had a very consistent schedule of time on and off the bike, the performance on the bike had some variability. What cannot be seen in the speed traces is the quality of sleep the rider received during each rest period. Our Masters winner had one rest block where he was unable to fall asleep and the consequences of that are readily apparent in the data, as has also been seen in the sports physiology literature.[10]

Figure 3.12 shows heart rate data for the second day of riding. While there was a lot of variability due to climbing and descending, the heart rate stayed largely above 100 bpm with an average of 105 bpm. The general trend of the heart rate starting around 115 bpm at the beginning of the day and slowly drifting downward as fatigue set in was a consistent trend throughout the race.

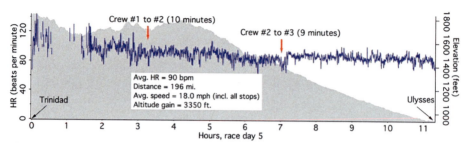

Figure 3.13. Heart rate for a relatively poor day of riding (5th shift), that followed a rest period with little or no sleep. The consistently low heart rate is indicative of fatigue. Note however that the crew exchanges had gotten much faster than in Figure 3.13, as the racer became very efficient with hygiene (Chapter 8), and the crew with their exchange tasks (Chapter 9).

Figure 3.13 tells a different story. On Day 5, during the ride from Trinidad, CO to Ulysses, KS, the average heart rate was just 90 bpm. The reason is very likely fatigue: at the end of Day 4, our racer deviated from his regular sleep cycle, and he was in the 'awake' phase of his circadian rhythm when he reached the motel (see Day 4/5 at the top of Figure 4.8). He reported lying awake most of the 4-hour rest period. This lack of sleep probably led to a substantially lower sustained heart rate and power output (Figure 3.13) on Day 5. It is worth noting in Figure 3.14 that it took the racer several days to recover fully from a single day of poor rest, although much of the recovery was achieved after the very next sleep. Despite having a setback in the middle of the race and suffering serious fatigue, returning to regular mid-day sleeping immediately allowed our racer to ride stronger every day as he approached the finish, while many other riders were likely suffering the effects of accumulated fatigue.

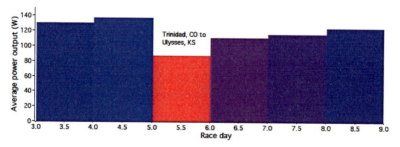

Figure 3.14. Power output by race day. The lowest power day on Day 5 followed a restless sleep period from which it took several days to recover fully.

Much more important than winning is safety. Day 5 was the only time that the Honey Badger fell asleep on the bike. Fortunately, he just drifted off towards the curb after he nodded off, rather than towards the center of the road. Nothing happened, but the crew got a good scare and made sure to chat with our racer frequently to keep him awake for the rest of the short way to Ulysses that day. Sadly, two racers have died during the long history of RAAM. We will never know for sure, but sleep deprivation may have played a role in these accidents. The regular sleep pattern that can be seen at the top of Figure 3.7 is likely to increase a racer's odds of survival above the statistical average of approximately 2 deaths per 200 finishers. In addition, night riding in follow mode is safer than leapfrogging during the day for a racer well-trained to ride at night. For these two reasons alone, we urge Masters racers to adopt our strategy. With the exception of Day 5, after a missed sleep period, our racer never had a problem staying awake during the entire race.

The bottom line of this chapter: Strategies that involve irregular and short sleep breaks work best for young riders. The Masters racers performed better with more regular sleep (higher Zs). The optimal sleep amount is about 2 REM cycles (L = 3.5 to 4 hours) per day. A 2 REM cycle/day strategy can also work for racers who have no trouble falling asleep quickly, like #583 in 2017. Just a single daily shift without sleep reduces performance[9] by about 20-30% (in terms of average heart rate and thus average output power), and requires at least 3 days of recovery (Figure 3.14). For that reason, regular sleep should be part of the racer's strategy **from day 1 of the race**. We recommend sleeping for the first time after about 20-22 hours, and not leaving out the first day's sleep break, as many of the racers in Figure 3.7 did. Jet-lagging yourself for mid-day sleep before the race is important to be able to sustain our strategy, which optimally matches the early afternoon RAAM start, and avoids much hot mid-day riding in favor of night riding. Some racers since 2016 tried our strategy, but were not able to sustain day sleep, perhaps because they had not adjusted their sleep schedule before the race. We also believe that regular sleep increases a racer's safety, and this is more important than any time gains.

4. RECENT RAAM RACES AND ALTERNATIVE STRATEGIES

In 2017 and 2018, several more riders adapted strategies similar to this book's. In particular, three sleep strategies emerged:

1. The classic 'sleep when you have to' strategy, marked by short and fairly irregular breaks.

2. The 'day sleep-night ride' strategy we discuss in this book, with variations of the sleep time.

3. A 'double nap' strategy that maintains regular sleep, but splits it into two shorter daytime and nighttime segments.

We will discuss examples of these in turn, and contrast them with less successful Masters strategies, as well as what the younger racers at the front of the field did.

Table 4.1. Rest variables for 2017 riders. T is the total race time in hours, L is the rest time in hours, L/T is the fraction of race time spent resting, Z signifies the regularity of the length of the rests, R signifies the regularity of the lengths of the rides, and D is the fraction of the rest taken during daytime hours (See table 3.1 for detailed explanation). The largest values of Z, R, and D are in bold.

	T	L	L/T	Z	R	D
Masters 1 (#500)	238.7	33.1	14%	1.5	2.2	46%
Masters 2 (#279)	252.2	39.3	16%	**2.2**	1.8	**76%**
Masters 3 (#443)	285.6	57.8	20%	1.8	**2.9**	57%
Masters 4 (#577)	285.6	62	22%	1.3	2.1	60%
Masters 5 (#301)	287.6	63.7	22%	1.2	1.2	38%
Overall 1 (#377)	201.6	14.9	7%	**3.3**	1.7	28%
Overall 2 (#349)	235.2	31.8	14%	1.9	2	13%
Overall 3 (#519)	242.9	28.1	12%	1.8	1.7	21%
Overall 4 (#583)	249.3	40.8	16%	2.8	**2.3**	**61%**
Overall 5 (#455)	263.4	61	23%	1.3	1.4	39%
Overall F 1 (#581)	282.9	51.3	18%	1.2	1.3	**55%**
Overall F 2 (#568)	292.6	39.3	13%	2	1.9	42%

Tables 4.1 and 4.2 show the rest variables for 2017 and 2018 riders. As pointed out already in Chapter 3, the two top Masters riders (both just turned 50) in 2017 rode on an amount of sleep between other Masters and Open winners of the race (~15% average), but the remaining top 5 male Masters came in with fractions of time slept L/T very similar to the top-performing Masters in

2016. Indeed, in 2018 the top three male Masters riders slept for an even larger fraction of the time (~25%) than the top Masters in 2016 and 2017. All of them finished slower than the top 3 in 2016. This may be partly due to weather differences and other matters out of their control, but we think they may have spent slightly too much time sleeping, thus eating into their overall time by 3-5%. Generally, the top performers ranked highest in at least some of the categories such as *Z* (sleep regularity) or *R* (ride regularity), or *D* (daytime sleep), but none combined high scores in all categories.

It is not trivial to implement our strategy of sleeping during the day. In 2017, #279 (Master) was able to use regular breaks in the late afternoon, and #558 slept very regular breaks during the day, fully implementing our strategy. However #577 tried day sleep, but reverted to night; #584 also tried day breaks, but ended up sleeping regular breaks at night or in the early morning hours. Our strategy requires sleeping 6 or more hours off one's normal sleep cycle. In 2016, the Honey Badger had to jet-lag himself by an hour a day for over a week before the start of the 2016 race to be able to do it. He also used ear plugs for each sleep period to mute any sound (after wearing them for weeks at night to get used to them), and drew dark shades. A sleeping mask (the type included in business class kits on long flights) could also be helpful to make sure the racer sleeps in darkness in the middle of the day. It would be easier for racers from Asia to implement our strategy because they are already lagged in the right direction when arriving to the race shortly before the start.

Table 4.2. Rest variables for 2018 riders.

	T	L	L/T	Z	R	D
Masters 1 (#602)	276.1	62.4	23%	1.7	**1.9**	**61%**
Masters 2 (#588)	281.7	73.6	26%	1.7	1.7	49%
Masters 3 (#411)	286.9	64.7	23%	**2.0**	1.6	48%
Masters F 1 (#161)	297.1	66.7	22%	1.5	1.4	**78%**
Masters F 5 (#415)	299.4	50.6	17%	**1.6**	**1.5**	46%
Gmasters 1 (#399)	305.5	60.4	20%	3.8	2	62%
Overall 1 (#377)	193.4	11.7	6%	**3.3**	1.3	34%
Overall 2 (#561)	228.6	51.1	22%	1.6	1.8	**57%**
Overall 3 (#592)	267.9	55.3	21%	2	**2.2**	32%
Overall F 1 (#549)	239.9	20.9	9%	2.1	2.2	55%

Interestingly, the top Open racer #377 has consistently high $Z = 3.3$ values in 2017 and 2018. He takes very few rests, but they are all very regular in length. He only took 9 breaks in 2018 above our duration threshold of >0.5

hours, and they averaged just 1.13 hours each, but he had the highest value of sleep regularity *Z*, higher even than the Honey Badger in 2016. Given the short sleep periods, the high *Z* value may not help much *per se*. Its correlation with winning may be more of an indication of a racer and crew capable of sticking to a carefully designed schedule, rather than riding with haphazard breaks. Iron discipline is certainly a winning attribute in RAAM.

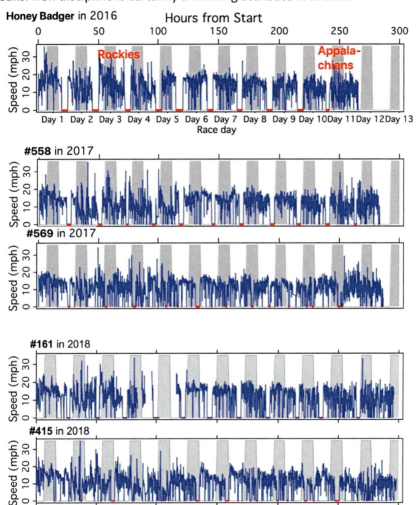

Figure 4.1 The Honey Badger's 2016 sleep strategy compared to other close races. In 2017, #558 and 569 were M Open racers from India (the 1st and 2nd to ever finish RAAM). In 2018, #161 and, 415) were F50-59 racers (1st and 2nd). Despite very similar output powers and neck-to-neck racing for the first 2000 miles, the regular day sleepers won both contests.

We now turn to a comparison of **(1)** pairs of close competitors in the same year, or **(2)** the same racer over a span of two years. Such comparisons are particularly useful because racers finishing with a similar time are more likely to have similar average output power, and strategy differences can make a big difference in their relative ranking; likewise, the same racer is likely to have similar output power in two consecutive years. For reference, Figure 4.1 also shows the Honey Badger's 2016 race at the top.

(1a) Two racers, #558 and #569, offer a particularly interesting anecdotal comparison in the 2017 race. Both of these racers were from India, and were the 1st and 2nd Indians to ever complete RAAM solo. #558 DNFd in 2016 on a very irregular sleep schedule. As can be seen in Figure 3.16, he adopted a regular daytime sleep strategy similar to the Honey Badger's in 2017. This racer was much younger than the Honey Badger, and slept only *ca.* 3 hours during the day instead of 4 hours. The other Indian racer, #569, adopted a much more irregular sleep strategy in 2017, with short night and daytime sleeps. Both racers have comparable average output power, as each finished in about 11-3/4 days. However, #558 with the more regular sleep schedule came in first.

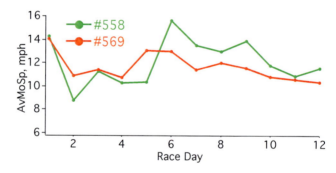

Figure 4.2 The average daily moving speeds (excluding sleep breaks) of #558, who adopted this book's sleep strategy, and #569, who did not.

Figure 4.2 shows why. The average speed (and presumably output power) of #558 in the first few days of the race was significantly lower than of #569, but then became significantly higher from days 6 through 12. We believe the main reason lies in #558's longer and more regular rest breaks in the middle of the day, which allowed him to recover from difficulties caused by the heat and altitude in the first few days of the race. Reduced fatigue at the end of the race produced a very similar result as Masters' 1st place *vs.* Masters 3d place in 2016: in both cases, the racer who slept regularly during the day was initially over 100 miles behind, but finally won by catching up and being hours ahead in Annapolis. That is why the strategy in this book requires courage to implement. You will likely be well behind similarly strong racers who ride with less sleep from the start, treating the race as though it were a three-day contest. Only past the Mississippi will you benefit from the reduced fatigue and forge ahead to victory.

(1b) In 2018, racers #161 and #415 in the women's Masters category offer a similar comparison because they finished within a few hours of one another. Racer #161, who DNFd on irregular sleep breaks in 2016, slept mostly during the day time ($D = 78\%$) for regular 2-3 hour intervals (see Figure 4.1). Racer #415 slept much later initially, and much less. While she was ahead for much of the race, she was caught by #161. We believe this is due to the extra boost at the end provided by longer and more regular rest breaks at the beginning. Our algorithm predicted a 12 day, 5 hour finish for #161, who ended up with 12 days, 9 hours. Paradoxically, we think it is possible that if #161 had slept longer (the 4+ hours in our algorithm rather than 2 hours in reality), she might have finished even faster than 12 days, 5 hours, all else being equal. In addition, more rest could have helped recovery from chafing and saddle pressure. At any rate, #161 in 2018 was a posterchild for the strategy we propose for Master's racers in this book, whether men or women.

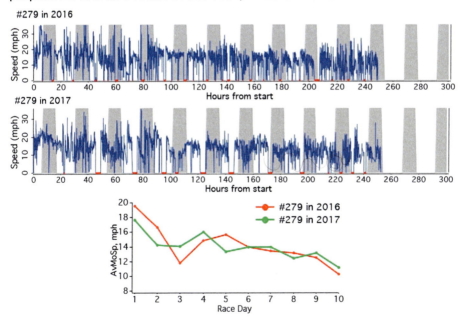

Figure 4.3 Speed vs. time plots and average daily moving speeds of #279 in 2016 and 2017.

(2) Racer #279 in Figure 4.3 offers another interesting comparison: same racer, two different sleep approaches in 2016 (Open 3rd) and 2017 (Masters 2nd). In 2016, #279 used regular short sleep breaks on a *ca.* 16 hour rotation schedule. In 2017, #279 used regular longer sleep breaks in the afternoon on a 24 hour rotation schedule, except he skipped the first break at 22 hours, and stopped several times on day 10. He finished in just under 250 hours in 2016, and in just over 250 hours in 2017, showing great consistency. The longer sleep schedule may have resulted in less of a dip in on-bike speed on day 3 (Figure 4.3, bottom panel), and slightly higher on-bike speed in the last two days. It is hard to say whether his 2017 race was a little slower due to the longer sleep breaks, due to not consistently following the strategy on the first and last day, or because conditions in 2017 were simply slightly tougher than 2016. (2017 and 2016 had similar ≈50% DNF rates.) Clearly though, good results can be obtained with the long sleep strategy even by someone who has proven many times over that he also can do very well with frequent short sleep breaks.

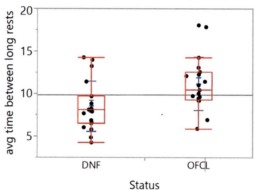

Figure 4.4 Average time in hours between long rests for Masters non-finishers (DNF, left) and official finishers (OFCL, right) in 2018. The probability that the difference is random is <5%.

The top goal at RAAM should be to finish, not DNF. A number of prominent racers in 2017 and 2018 DNFd either because of illness (e.g. respiratory infection or edema), or because of bike crashes (possibly caused by excessive fatigue). Successful racers tend to have longer and more regular riding periods between rest periods. In particular, successful Masters racers had on average about 3 hour longer riding periods between rest periods than those who DNFd (Figure 4.4). We do not find such a strong correlation for younger racers who slept irregularly or had shorter rides between breaks. We surmise that some of the Masters DNF racers would have avoided illness or crashes, had they followed the "regular sleep during the day - long ride at night" strategy of this book. Only if they were to make a direct comparison, like #558 did in

2016/2017, or #161 did in 2017/2018, would we be able to tell whether our strategy can help convert their racing from DNF to a solid finish.

Double-Napping – A Variation of the Strategy

Several racers, from first time finishers to those with a record number of participations, have successfully adapted our strategy to their needs. Yet some racers may find two aspects of our 'sleep long during the day-ride fast at night' strategy daunting: the nearly uninterrupted hours in the saddle each day (up to 20+); and sleeping sufficiently long and well during the day, which requires jet-lagging. A few solo racers have solved this conundrum with a variation of our strategy, which may not be as efficient for some riders, but works for other riders: double-napping.

The idea is to distribute the sleep break into two shorter but regular breaks. One break remains in the middle of the day, and splits the hot day riding in half, albeit with about two fewer hours of sleep and thus two more hours of riding in the heat. The other break shifts to the middle of the night. Together, the two sleep breaks sum up to the *ca.* 4 hours we recommend for Masters, or less for younger racers more tolerant of sleep deprivation. The important factor is that the most successful practitioners still slept very regularly, i.e. the two breaks where not of haphazard timing and duration.

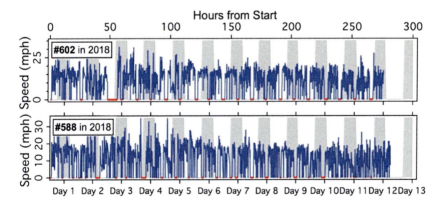

Figure 4.5 The top two Masters racers in 2018 followed a 'double-napping' (top) or 'irregular' (bottom) strategy. They were neck-to-neck most of the race, but the regular double-napper won the Masters title in 2018.

Figure 4.5 illustrates the strategy with actual data from Master racers #602 in and #588 in 2018. #602 attempted pure day sleep on days 1 and 2, and then switched over to take a shorter break every 12 hours, one at night and one in the middle of the day. #588 followed a more irregular sleep strategy. The two racers tracked each other for most of the race, but towards the end, the regular 'double-napper' forged ahead to Masters victory. Most remarkably, #602 has type I diabetes. Just finishing RAAM is an immense accomplishment that requires an extremely controlled feeding and hydration schedule and constant monitoring. Having two daily breaks instead of one may have helped with execution by providing a second long pause for checking in on the racer's status.

The bottom line of Chapter 4: Recent RAAM results confirm that regular day sleep and night riding can take racers from a DNF one year to a Masters win the next, or beat the competition at the end of the race when it counts, as long as the two riders have comparable power output. An interesting variation on the strategy, for racers who have a tough time sleeping exclusively during the day and doing one long riding shift, is to take two sleep breaks on a regular schedule, one during the day, and one at night. The two breaks still should add up to about 4 hours for a Masters racer (less for younger Open racers).

5. PRE-RACE **PREPARATION** – THE RACER

RAAM is a very demanding single-stage, multi-day race. The implementation of our race plan requires careful racer preparation (this chapter) and crew preparation (next chapter). The Honey Badger allotted nearly three and a half years, from January 2013 to May 2016, for training. Some of the training addressed **keystones 1 to 3** of our strategy (night riding, proper length of sleep breaks, very long riding shifts); some of the training addressed aerobic performance and endurance, as any training plan for RAAM should do. We discuss all the racer-related aspects in this chapter, and turn to the crew in the next.

The Honey Badger's training included shorter races to keep up motivation in successive years: Two-person RAAM for solo RAAM qualification in 2013 (1500 miles), ten Ironman triathlons in 2014 (1407 miles total), a brevet week and Paris-Brest-Paris in 2015 (1530 miles total). The time between races was spent doing a lot of aerobic threshold training, a little interval training, and some 'just ride and burn fat' time in the saddle. This chapter summarizes the various stages of the training, and provides some numbers as guidance for the RAAM Masters racer. Of key importance is calibrating the length of your daily sleep, which turned out to be 4 hours (nod-off time plus roughly 2 REM cycles) for The Honey Badger. The key is to get some deep sleep, and wake up when sleep is light.

Training Plan

Martin decided early on to test Phil Maffetone's program of mainly aerobic threshold training (HR ≈ 180 – age, ±5 beats, or 125 to 135 beats for a 50-year old), based on advice from his trainer Sarah Young, and real-life long-term tests he carried out.

In the period between 2010 and 2012, Martin had followed a rigorous interval training program to compete in ultracycling races, marathons, and Ironman triathlons: Alternating running all-out 400 meters with 1200 meter recovery, to repeat in the next mile; or riding a mile all-out on the bike, then recovering for two miles and repeating until the mile speed dropped more than 10%. And so forth. The program paid off with a podium at the Rev 3 Ironman distance race, a course record of 8:47 (co-held with Collin Johnson) at the Metamora 200 mile ultracycling race, and *ca.* 7:15/mi. PR at the Boston Marathon with under 35 miles of run training per week. Martin was running a 6:45/mi. pace at 130 beats per minute between miles 3 and 4 of a 4-mile run. However, the interval training also brought problems: frequent small overuse injuries, such as shinbone stress fractures that required MRI diagnosis, an Achilles tendon that had to be scraped painfully, and undiagnosed arch and hip pain, to name but a few. Constant small injuries, and the necessary training breaks they require, are not compatible with a RAAM training schedule, where the racer has to put in long hours and large mileage consistently every week to acclimatize to race conditions.

Martin's sister had given him the "Big Book of Endurance Racing" by Phil Maffetone as a coffee-table book, and it was ignored for a while. But during idle winter days, while recovering from an overuse injury, Martin read it, and was intrigued: the book promised gains almost as good as interval training, while riding and running injury-free at the aerobic threshold (around 180-age = 130 bpm for a 50-year-old Master ultracyclist). The downside was that it would take longer to get the results. The approach had taken Ironman-great Paul Allen to Kona victory. So Martin decided to put the claims made by Maffetone to a long-term test three years before RAAM.

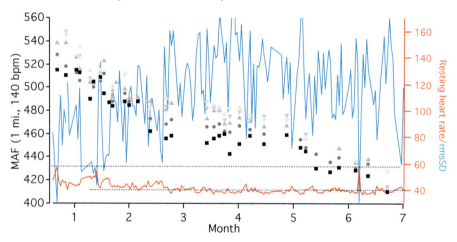

Figure 5.1 Effect of aerobic threshold training over 6 months. Plotted are: Aerobic pace (at 130-135 beats per minute, from mile 1 (black square) to mile 5 (gray diamond), resting heart rate (red curve) and heart rate root-mean-squared standard deviation (rmsSD, blue curve). Note that the resting heart rate dropped from the low 50s to high 30s during this 6-month training stretch, rmsSD increased from an average around 80-100 milliseconds to 120-140 milliseconds, and pace at 130-135 bpm dropped from over 9 minutes/mile to under 7 minutes/mile, all very notable improvements.

Having rested in the winter because of an overuse injury, Martin's pace between miles 3 to 4 of a 130 bpm four-mile run had slowed down to about

9:05/mile, or a "Maximum Aerobic Function" ("MAF") of 545 seconds/mile. For 6 months, Martin would bike and run only up to his aerobic threshold (135 beats per minute), without any interval training. As can be seen in Figure 5.1, the fourth-mile pace decreased from 9:05/mile to a "MAF" of 415 seconds/mile or a 6:55/mile over 6+ months. This is quite a respectable improvement, and Martin was able to run half marathons in just over 1:27, and full marathons in just over 3:10 at age 50. Although interval training could have pushed these times down even further, Martin had been free of pain or injury for over 6 months. He decided to keep up the aerobic threshold training, especially because RAAM does not require any sprinting or sudden accelerations, thanks to its 9+ day time table for Masters racers.

Table 5.1 Training plan from 2013 to 2016 to prepare for RAAM. The key points are: 1) major races as milestones to motivate training; 2) early on, a combination of cycling, running and swimming to build core and legs. 3) only cycling for the last half year; 4) periodization with lower intensity periods both on an annual and on a monthly basis. BEM = Bike equivalent mileage is simply calculated as (Cycling mileage) + 3 x (Run mileage) + 10 x (Swim mileage). BEM provides a rough guide to how much pure cycle training would be required to obtain about the same aerobic conditioning as provided by the plan in Table 5.1.

Month	Monthly mileages				Major Endurance Races (> 3 hours)
	Cycle	Run	Swim	BEM	
Jan. 2013	602	127	8	1063	-
Feb. 2013	617	136	9	1115	-
Mar. 2013	789	148	9	1323	-
April 2013	865	98	10	1259	Boston Marathon
May 2013	1501	16	8	1630	-
June 2013	2013	20	4	2111	RAAM 2-man, M25-49
July 2013	861	83	10	1210	-
Aug. 2013	927	125	10	1402	Great Illini Half Ironman
Sept. 2013	665	94	9	1037	-
Oct. 2013	749	128	10	1233	Beach to Battleship Iron race
Nov. 2013	511	124	8	963	-
Dec. 2013	551	93	9	920	Ironman Cozumel, CA Intl' Marathon
Jan. 2014	528	141	7	1021	-
Feb. 2014	526	142	8	1032	-
Mar. 2014	708	151	11	1271	Ironman Los Cabos
April 2014	761	139	9	1268	Calvin's Challenge 12 h
May 2014	925	109	11	1362	Ironman Texas
June 2014	843	130	10	1333	Ironman Cairns
July 2014	979	69	11	1296	Ironman Coeur d'Alene, Fat Ass 12-hour
Aug. 2014	801	100	12	1221	Ironman Boulder, Ironman Louisville
Sept. 2014	701	106	9	1109	Ironman Wisconsin, Ironman Maryland

Oct. 2014	669	148	8	1193	-
Nov. 2014	623	137	10	1134	Ironman Cozumel
Dec. 2014	516	111	8	929	-
Jan. 2015	460	146	12	1018	-
Feb. 2015	612	46	7	816	-
Mar. 2015	938	2	7	1016	-
April 2015	1051	2	10	1157	Calvins' Challenge 12h race, 300k brevet
May 2015	1323	37	10	1534	Brevet week – 760 miles
June 2015	1044	52	10	1300	-
July 2015	1118	60	10	1398	Fat Ass 6h ultracycling race
Aug. 2015	1329	28	12	1533	Paris – Brest – Paris 780 miles
Sept. 2015	721	57	8	972	Ironman Chattanooga
Oct. 2015	608	0	0	608	(low mileage due to multiple fractures)
Nov. 2015	941	17	1	1002	-
Dec. 2015	1014	12	5	1100	-
Jan. 2016	1202	0	0	1202	-
Feb. 2016	1263	1	0	1266	-
Mar. 2016	1569	0	0	1569	RAAM crew test race – 350 miles
April 2016	1489	0	0	1489	-
May 2016	2121	0	0	2121	-
June 2016	3330	0	0	3330	RAAM Solo, M50-59 Division

In practice, the training time consisted of about 40% aerobic threshold (180-age ± 5 beats), 5% intervals above the aerobic threshold, and 55% fat burning below the aerobic threshold. The intervals resulted from training with crit racers at club rides, never from fast running, which is much more likely to lead to an overuse injury than cycling. Even for a RAAM racer, some interval training is probably a good idea to push up the VO_2max more efficiently. The 55% slow riding happened on warm-ups, warm-downs and long rides. It was not a complete waste of time: Although slow riding did not improve the aerobic threshold or VO_2max, it allowed many of the saddle tests, sleep tests (**keystone 1** of our strategy) and nutrition tests to be carried out. Slow riding also accommodated the racer mentally to spending long, uninterrupted hours on the saddle (**keystone 3** of our strategy). A RAAM racer pressed for training time could probably cut a good fraction of that slow riding out of their training schedule, and still perform very well. But do not do this at the cost of not understanding your sleep or saddle needs.

With the efficacy of long-term aerobic threshold training established, the Honey Badger followed a periodized training schedule though the years 2013-2016. At first the schedule emphasized range of motion (Sarah Young is Original Strength certified), running, and triathlon competitions equally with cycling, to provide general aerobic training and keep the body's core in good shape (Table 5.1). The training schedule finally migrated to long cycling sessions exclusively in the last 7 months before RAAM to train the legs more race-specifically. The training was successful: Martin never suffered significant neck or back pain during the race, and the legs remained completely free of soreness after 11 days of solo RAAM. The table shows a month-by-month summary of the training and the races integrated into training, leading up to solo RAAM.

The BEM (Bike Equivalent Mileage) value in Table 5.1 is to provide the pure cyclist with an approximate reference for equivalent aerobic effort on the bike. Typically, running speed is about 3x slower at the same heart rate, and swimming is about 10x slower at the same heart rate than cycling. Thus BEM reflects the monthly training load in a single number, roughly proportional to the amount of time spent training, which varied from 10 hours/week during certain winter months to 25 hours/week during certain summer months.

As one can see, the effort dropped below a BEM of 1000 miles only a couple of months per year, usually in the late fall (in the early fall during the last annual training cycle). Conversely, monthly mileages never increased above 1500 miles except during race months (RAAM 2-man in June 2013, brevet week in May 2015, and Paris-Brest-Paris in August 2015), and for the last few months before RAAM. Then the racer ramped up mileage from 1000 miles in December 2015 to over 2000 miles in May 2016, before tapering for RAAM in the first two weeks of June. The Honey Badger does well on a relatively short taper, and finds 'leg memory' to be better when no more than 2 weeks pass without significant cycling mileage before a big race.

Within a given month, the training followed a typical periodization, with a week of very high mileage (*e.g.* 100-120-220-120 rides, or 248-127-372 rides, for example) followed by a week of less mileage (200 miles), surrounded by two weeks of average mileage (250 to 300 miles). Rather than following a strict period, the Honey Badger simply integrated low volume weeks somewhat randomly with travel required by work, not riding on days of plane travel, while giving lectures at conferences, or when severely jet-lagged. This is not optimal, but practical for racers with a work schedule outside of racing. For a long race like RAAM (over 3000 miles), with a long training schedule (over 3 years), irregularity in periodization probably has little effect on performance, as long as regular rest during training and the taper at the end are not neglected.

Compression Gear

One item that proved extremely helpful during training were thigh-length medical compression socks, available from any medical or hospital supply store for about $40 a pair. While not very appealing to the eye, these socks provided excellent compression during long travel periods or other periods of low mobility. Martin tested recovery after rides for 2 months without, and 2 months with socks on every day for at least 9 hours. The objective report based on recovery of resting heart rate (as low as possible) and heart rate root-mean-square fluctuation (as high as possible, see Figure 5.1) after similar exertions is that recovery was much better with the socks, which also kept varicose vein symptoms at bay. For Masters racers, varicose veins induced by cycling shorts are always looming, and if for no other reason, the compression socks were worth every penny spent.

Training Races and Qualification Races

Table 5.1 contains a major race or series of races for every year of RAAM training leading up to the 2016 RAAM:

2013: Two-man Team RAAM (*ca.* 1500 miles in one segment)
2014: 10 Ironman races for the season (*ca.* 1400 miles in 10 segments)
2015: A brevet week and Paris – Brest – Paris (*ca.* 1500 miles in 2 segments).

Each of these units was handled in a specific way to provide the desired results. Aspiring RAAM racers and veterans alike are highly encouraged to integrate at least one full 1500 mile racing unit into every year preceding RAAM. First of all, it provides motivation for training, which can sometimes be hard to come by when the grand goal is years in the future. More importantly, the races provide important RAAM-like tests, as described next.

Two-man Team RAAM: The Honey Badger rode this race with his friend and future crew member Jay Yost, finishing third behind two Danish teams in 7 days and 4 hours. Jay and Martin decided to race in a completely unorthodox fashion, which would probably cost some time, but serve a greater purpose: preparation for the conditions of solo RAAM. Most two-person teams alternate 1- to 2-hour shifts during the day with 4- to 6-hour shifts at night, to get some reasonable night rest and keep the legs fresh during the day. An RV for the racers is *de rigeur* for those seeking a podium, allowing one racer to rest until the start of his or her next shift, while the other one is on the road.

Instead, Jay and Martin each had their own three-person crew, with a single crew vehicle. They each rode a 12-hour shift of 190-240 miles each day, slept in a hotel for 4 hours at the end of their shift together with their personal crew, then drove and shopped with their crew for 8 hours to catch the other racer at the next exchange. Jay, with his higher output power and heavier build took on the night shift. Martin, at 143 pounds (65 kg) a very heat-resistant and fast climber, took on the day shift and the race's major climbs over Wolf Creek Pass, the Ozarks, and the Appalachians.

The race thus provided a rather good simulation of the RAAM strategy espoused in this book, with long riding shifts and regular sleep breaks, one each per race day. The only concession was that an additional seven hours of solo RAAM riding each day was replaced by driving around with the crew. This approach put considerable strain on the racers (and the single crew per racer), but it demonstrated convincingly that a long-sleep, long-ride schedule could be kept up for a week, and lead to a very good finish time even in the two-man team race.

Jay Yost and Martin Gruebele crossing the official finish line of two-man team RAAM in 2013, after 7d 4h of racing. They rode mainly 12-hour shifts with 3 to 4 hours of sleep, to test their future solo RAAM strategy.

Martin's sustainable heart rate dropped from *ca.* 125 beats per minute on days 1 and 2, to 110 bpm on Day 7. Hence the estimate that about 100 to 110 beats or HR=160-age would be sustainable in solo RAAM. This estimate proved to be achievable during solo RAAM whenever the racer was well-rested (4 hours/day) and caffeinated, although the average heart rate during the Honey Badger's solo RAAM was closer to 100. The two-man race also showed that a four-hour sleep break was really necessary for Martin. When he had a shorter break after Day 3 of the two-man team race after riding almost 14 hours instead of 12, his heart rate and performance dropped drastically on the ride across Kansas. When he then slept 4 hours again, the performance went back up the following day. A REM cycle (going from deep sleep to light sleep to REM sleep) is about 90 minutes, so 4 hours is sufficient for just over two cycles, including the time needed to fall asleep. Thus, two-man team RAAM is a very useful place to gauge the length of the sustainable sleep break. It may be less than 2 hours for the world's best young riders, like Strasser or Bischoff, but it will be about 4 hours for the Masters rider. Extensive experimentation (see also below) is very important here, and it is better to overestimate the needed sleep by a half hour, than to underestimate it. The latter has dire consequences a few days into the race, as it clearly did for the Honey Badger's competitor from Denmark, an experienced RAAM racer who was in the lead for several days on very little sleep, but later fatigued, fell back, and ended up having to sleep more than our racer during the second half of the race.

Here's an example of one of the many small but useful things the Honey Badger learned during two-man team RAAM in 2013. He rode that race without protecting his forearms. By the end of Day 6, the area below the elbow was so chafed from sweating in the aerobars, that it had become impossible to place the arm in the aero position. The crew had to apply a surgical skin replacement and fasten it around the arm with a piece of tape so Martin could continue to ride in the aerobars. A simple solution to this problem that worked perfectly during solo RAAM, is to wear white compression sleeves, which also serve as forearm protectors. Martin wore them all the time during RAAM in 2016, and never chafed his arms the tiniest bit, even though he was on the bike more than twice as long as in 2013.

In addition to allowing the racer to figure out many small and large tricks, the two-person team race served as a qualifier for RAAM. A similar combination of calibration and qualification could be achieved by racing RAW, or certain multi-day ultraraces in Europe. For many aspiring RAAM racers these are also a good stepping stone for solo RAAM. However, the two-man race is even longer than these, and a more realistic gauge of performance, and is strongly recommended by the authors. For example, nutrition problems do not really surface until the third or fourth day, so RAW will not provide a reliable guide of what to expect during RAAM. If two-man team RAAM is attempted, it should be done on the long-ride, long-sleep schedule. The conventional approach does little to prepare one properly for RAAM, and fails to provide performance numbers that can be translated into RAAM performance.

Our strategy for two-man RAAM, besides being useful as RAAM training and qualification, does have one major advantage over the conventional strategy:

simplicity. There is only one crew and crew vehicle per racer, and the schedule is identical each day: ride 12 hours, be relieved by the other racer, sleep 4 hours in a hotel, then drive about 200 miles with one's crew to catch up and restock, and relieve the other racer and crew. Racers who can sleep in the car while their crew is driving can even get more rest than just the 4 hours at the hotel. It is a strain on the crew to sleep only about 4 hours each day, which is why the Honey Badger used three 8 hour crews for solo RAAM in 2016. However, especially if you relieve a start crew member in each crew with a fresh replacement around the Mississippi, you can get on the two-person podium (we did) or possibly even win with our two-man strategy. Just make sure to get your start crew to the finish line to celebrate with you!

Ironman bike rides are quite short at 112 miles, but running a marathon afterwards provides plenty of fatigue resistance and aerobic training value. The swim-bike-run combination is excellent cross-training for ultracyclists interested in a strong core.

Ironman: The year of 10 Ironmans in 2013/2014 provided a racing mileage similar to two-man team RAAM, but cut up into much shorter one-day events. The races mainly provided motivation for extensive aerobic cycling-running-swimming training in 2014. A pure cyclist could simply substitute a series of 12-hour and 200-mile ultracycling races, if running and swimming are not up their alley. The Honey Badger did several of those also. However, the cross-training in 2014 brought about a significant strengthening of the core muscles, and made it possible for the Honey Badger to absolve 750+ mile cycling weeks without a sore back, shoulders, neck or arms. This is the main utility of cross-training into other endurance disciplines, and we strongly recommend that aspiring RAAM racers give it a try, unless a physical problem prevents them from running or swimming or weight exercises. Besides, Ironman races are relatively speaking "easy" compared to multi-day ultracycling races.[†] The Honey Badger climbed to an Ironman 7/2000 M50-54 US age group ranking in 2014, and a 19/6000 world ranking, and so can other RAAM racers, with much less damage to their training schedule than is caused by a single 24-hour ultracycling race.

Avoid 24 hour races for training: Speaking of 24-hour races: against conventional wisdom, we strongly recommend that Masters racers *not* do too many 24-hour ultracycling races as part of their solo RAAM training plan. Martin tried them pre-2013, and they proved enormously disruptive to his training schedule. The problem is that a racer with a strong circadian rhythm will really suffer from not going to sleep for well over 24 hours. The minimum of 27 waking hours that includes early morning race preparation and the awards ceremony can quickly turn into 48 waking hours if you can't fall asleep after the awards ceremony. The 24+ hour situation does not actually arise during a well-planned solo RAAM when one is following the strategy in this book. Thus, there is absolutely no reason to train for it. The Honey Badger required 2 weeks of recovery (judged by resting heart rate and heart rate variation) after 24-hour races because he missed up to 48 hours of sleep. That recovery was highly disruptive of his training schedule, and with no real training value for a racer who plans to average 20 hours of riding and 3 to 4 hours of sleeping every day. This is to be compared with 2 days of recovery after 12-hour races. You should do 24-hour races only because you like that race format, need one to qualify for RAAM, or you can fall asleep anytime/anywhere – in which case the strategy in this book may not be the best for you.

Brevet week and Paris-Brest-Paris (P-B-P): For the final year before RAAM, Martin chose two 750+ mile "race" weeks as the best training motivator to get ready for solo RAAM, without doing races so exhausting that they would require more than a week of recovery (a problem with two-man team RAAM).

[†] Of course, triathlon has its own crazy multi-day races, such as doing 10 Ironmans in 10 days, or an event where one races 10 times the Ironman distance for each segment without an official break, i.e. a 24 mile swim, 1120 mile bike ride, and 262 mile run.

Randonneurs USA (RUSA) organizes many timed rides, called brevets. The same is true for randonneuring organizations in other countries, including all over Europe, Japan, and even in India and China. Qualification by a brevet series can culminate in one of the Grand Randonnées, such as P-B-P (held every four years). P-B-P conveniently was on the calendar in 2015, but there are many other 1200k+ brevets in the US, England (London-Edinburgh), and elsewhere. Moreover, the front of a randonnée like P-B-P is just like a bicycle race: competitors are interested in breezing as quickly as possible through time stations (called "Contrôles" for brevets).

The start lineup at a typical brevet, Quad City Randonneurs 300k in Iowa. Besides some hard riding from time station to time station, there is a lot of camaraderie and trading of war stories, as randonneuring is a bit more sociable than ultraracing – a welcome diversion. Two of the other participants (Dave and Tom) were RAAM veterans or RAAM qualifiers, so there is usually strong company for a hard push to the finish. During brevet week, many racers serious about P-B-P qualification are also at hand the year before and the year of P-B-P.

The key for the RAAM racer in training was to ride the long P-B-P randonnée like solo RAAM. Martin remained on US time while in France, to make riding at night and sleeping in the middle of the day easy. He rode at Paris-Brest-Paris for 22 hours during the night (**keystone 3**), slept for 2 hours in the middle of the day (**keystone 2**), then rode 33 more hours to the finish, to simulate a situation that could arise at the end of solo RAAM. He finished 7/441 US randonneurs with this strategy. The 2-hour sleep period (half the planned sleep for RAAM) was unsustainably short for solo RAAM, but it proved that a shorter sleep, and skipping one sleep period at the end, was a feasible end game for solo RAAM. This has also been found in physiological studies of "shorter" (600 kilometer) ultracycling events.[6] Incidentally, by using this strategy Martin finished about 10 hours ahead of two riding buddies with demonstrated equal or higher output power, who chose a minimal/irregular sleep strategy, and who slept at night instead of during the day. This provides additional evidence that maintaining a regular 24-hour sleep rhythm during multi-day races and sleeping during the hot daytime hours can be beneficial, even for racers who have no trouble falling asleep at any time.

One organized series of rides, which the Honey Badger did to prepare for P-B-P, is a 'brevet week.' During a brevet week, the 200-300-400-600k brevets required to qualify for P-B-P are all held in a row, also conducive to a 1200k+ (750+ mile) ride. Martin rode this brevet week with crew member Jay Yost and cycling friend Ryan Linne in four days. That is somewhat below the RAAM or P-B-P intensity, but still quite a workout for the year before RAAM solo. Getting the brevet booklet stamped at time stations, and receiving the qualification for P-B-P, also resulted in quite a bit of satisfaction and motivation. Thus brevets and randonnées can also be recommended from a mental preparation point of view.

Long randonnées, like the 1200 kilometer = 780 mile P-B-P above, provide excellent opportunities for night riding under race-like conditions.

For ultraracers not interested in randonnées, there are of course plenty of good races to substitute: the Silver State 508, the Dolomitica, the Tortour, RAW, or one of many other US and European medium-distance races in the

500-900 mile range that have major climbs. Doing two of these provides a RAAM-like experience as well as confidence in the year before the big one.

Gauging Your Need for Sleep

One of the most important elements of RAAM preparation is to settle the length of your sleep break. It would be nice if there were a simple formula, but individual racers react very differently to sleep deprivation. As a general rule though, while the best 30-year-old racers in the Open male category can sustain sleep breaks of one REM cycle per day (*ca.* 90 minutes) for 8 or 9 days, the best Masters racers will need at least 2 REM cycles (*ca.* 3 hours) for 10 to 11 days.

The Honey Badger found out, via various length sleep breaks at two-man team RAAM, that 3 hours were insufficient, but 4 hours were enough to sustain a >100 beat per minute heart rate day after day. The reason is most likely that it takes our racer about a half hour to fall deeply asleep, and so waking up before 3.5 hours is difficult. This was confirmed in 2014 and 2015 by trying three or four successive days of long (130- to 250-mile) training rides with varying amounts of sleep: get up at 3 AM after 3 hours of sleep, or at 4 AM after 4 hours of sleep, and see what happens after three days of such a routine. Invariably, 4 hours turned out to lead to sustainable performance over 4 days, but 3 hours did not.

This conclusion is supported by a previous study on a RAAM team that found dramatically improved quality of sleep for rest periods longer than 3 hours compared to rest periods shorter than 3 hours,[11] likely because the body adapts to persistent sleep deprivation.[12] Martin tended to wake up more easily on his own after 4 hours than after 3 hours. The REM part of sleep is a sweet spot for waking up and feeling fresh instead of groggy. We all tend to wake up more easily while dreaming, rather than wake up from deep sleep. This sweet spot may vary from racer to racer, but it is a very important one to determine for yourself, and the main reason why the two-man team RAAM is strongly recommended as a test race in this book. As discussed in Chapter 9, the crew used a special procedure to wake up the Honey Badger during that sweet spot, neither too early nor too late.

The goal for the Masters racer is straightforward: sleep enough to be able to ride as fast on-bike as the Open male winner, which means about 7.5 days on-bike for the strongest Masters winners, and about 8.5 days on-bike time for an average Masters winning performance. The difference between the Masters winner and the Open male winner should be the amount of sleep required, not the moderate average speed ridden, which is well within the ability of any ultracycling racer (see Chapter 3).

An important side effect of a "long" (4-hour) sleep block is improved digestion. Irregular sleep promotes irregular bowel movements and incomplete digestion because the digestive system never gets the blood flow it needs during the race. This is especially true for Masters athletes. If you intend to eat "real" food during the race (the Honey Badger ate a sandwich during most crew shifts, and one more food item like pizza or pasta just before the rest break every day), a 4-hour sleep break is imperative. While it may be possible to synthesize glycogen in some inactive muscle fiber types during exercise, rest is necessary to replenish glycogen in the cycling-active muscles.[13] The reward for adequate sleep will be improved glycogen storage.[14] Ignoring the needs of your digestive system will simply cause you to bonk after 2 to 3 days, as Martin found out by testing 3-hour sleep breaks in the years before the race.

Testing Your Equipment and Clothing

Another key item during solo RAAM preparation is saddle choice.[15] Unless you have already ridden 200-200-200-200 mile back-to-back days and found saddles that work for you, you need to dedicate the full three years to your quest for the best saddles. Note that we use the plural here, "saddles." The reason is that riding a mix of saddles during the race on a daily basis changes the pressure points, and delays that unavoidable moment when riding becomes painful at the sitbone pressure points. After years of riding long distances, the Honey Badger settled on the Selle Italia SLK (relatively soft and split), the Selle San Marco Zoncolan (relatively hard but a good sit bone shape) and the SQlabs 612 (which cradles you like two hands). Many others fell by the wayside: Selle San Marco Aspide, Selle Italia SLR, Adamo ISM, Terry and Brooks; the list goes on and on. Do not take the above examples in any way as an endorsement of rejection of any of these saddles: seating is very idiosyncratic, and depends on the sit bone geometry, spacing between the thighs, and racer weight. We wish we could give better advice than to try out a variety of saddles during 500+ mile races, but trial and error it is. There are some general guidelines, however: Do measure your sit bone spacing (13 cm for the Honey Badger, so the SQlabs 612 13 cm fit nicely), and choose among saddles that match it. Pick saddles with a dimple or a split in the right place, it can truly help reduce numbness. And at all cost select saddles that have a narrow nose, and perhaps even hold a nose-free saddle in reserve (the Honey

Badger did not). Chafing of the inner thigh is a slow but insidious process if the nose is too wide. It was the major source of pain for our racer by Day 10 of the race.

Here is a key tip for good saddle positioning. Have someone observe you from behind while riding at an 18 mph pace. If you slide even ever so slightly (> 1 cm) back and forth sideways on your saddle when viewed from the rear, you need to dial in your position better. The seam on the Honey Badger's bibs does not budge sideways more than a few millimeters during riding, reducing the chafing that comes with rubbing your bibs across the saddle surface. As a result, the Honey Badger did not become fidgety until Day 11, when even the slightest bit of chafing finally took its toll.

The same strategy goes for bib shorts. First of all, Martin rode bib shorts, not regular shorts. While bibs may be less convenient during kit change (the jersey has to be removed), the shoulder straps reduce chamois shifting, and prevent slippage that could get the lower back severely burned. The lower back is an area where it is all too easy to forget the daily morning routine of applying sunscreen, and heavy sweating, or crews spraying you with water in the Arizona desert, will wash off the sunscreen on your back. Your jersey will invariably ride up your back, exposing it, with dire consequences. Sunburn can drastically increase the feeling of fatigue the racer experiences, as happened to Martin in 2013 at two-man team RAAM. For 2016, the Honey Badger bought 8 brands/styles of bib shorts, ranging from $45 to $345. He tested them on multiple 200-mile rides, until it became clear which ones felt ever so slightly more comfortable, did not wad up in the wrong places, and remained tolerable when wet or sweaty. Three clear winners emerged, ranging from expensive Assos shorts to rather inexpensive Giordana shorts. It's a very personal question of the shape of your seating area, but the key philosophy is: give each of your three crews one of your favorite bib shorts, and make sure to change them at each crew exchange on hot race days. A single short for the day will suffice on cooler days. Likewise, a bib change is not necessary after the night shift, when sweating is minimal. Martin changed bibs almost every day between the sweaty afternoon and cooler evening shifts.

Your race shoes are no less important. The Honey Badger ended up riding for the most part the well-worn Shimano touring shoes he rode during the 2013 two-man team RAAM because they had proven themselves. He got hotfoot on his left foot after wearing a newer but also extensively tested pair of shoes, feeling numb in one toe for weeks after the race. Fortunately, this was the extent of the damage. Based on experience, if you ride 100-200-150 mile sequences on successive days, and wearing the same shoes give you the slightest bit of discomfort, search for other shoes. We recommend the following in general: Get shoes with simple Velcro straps, instead of complex buckle or wheel mechanisms, which are hard to operate when you are fatigued after 8 days. Get shoes that are 2 European sizes larger than a nice snug race fit for ordinary day-long races. Your feet will swell in the heat, and a loose toe box and a slight loss of power are nothing compared to fully developed hotfoot. The Honey Badger got European size 45 instead of 43. And finally, mount your cleats fairly far back on the shoes – some racers even go so far as to drill extra holes further back. The reason is that the nerve endings that sense feeling in your toes are quite sensitive to pressure at the front of your foot, and you will lose feeling from the endless pedaling (so-called hotfoot). At a cadence of 80 rpm, riding 19 hours a day, you will put in over a million pedal strokes during RAAM. Put some of that pressure a little further back than the ball of your foot, even though you would never dream of doing so in a short 12-hour race.

The last physical element of your race is racer electronics. Use your favorite system from Garmin, Polar, or whomever, but we believe that smartphone battery life and features have progressed to where it becomes an able substitute. The Honey Badger used a smartphone mounted in a phone bento box for multiple purposes: to display a map and provide voice cues via a single earbud; to play music or audiobooks through the same earbud for entertainment; to collect heart rate data and display it for immediate feedback; and for emergency communication with the crew during leapfrogging. All this is described in more detail in Chapter 7. Here the important message is to train with the equipment you will use for at least 6 months, under all possible conditions: extreme heat, rain, at night, during the day. It is very important for the racer to know all the operations of their GPS/audio/map/communications devices in his or her sleep because that is practically how they will have to be operated later in the race. We found out, for example, that the smartphone overheats in the direct sun, and needs to be put inside the bento box or in the jersey back pocket. Either way, the voice GPS cues still work. Smart phones are also going to be around for a while to come, while the 'sports gadget of the day' comes and goes.

Training and Measures to Cope With Monotony

Ultracyclist Amanda Coker rode a *ca.* 7 mile loop over 200 miles each day for 365 days to set her 86,000+ miles annual mileage record in 2017. She bested

Tommy Godwin's famous 1939 record by over 11,000 miles. Never mind that her equipment is more modern, or the weather in Florida may be better than in England: how does someone conquer the demons of boredom and monotony for such a feat? Our task is a much smaller one during RAAM, but a tough task nonetheless, which can lead to a DNF for unprepared racers.

Perhaps the most important mental element of the race is dealing with 18 to 22 hours of monotony each day, especially while riding at night. No matter what music, no matter what scenery, the monotony will become difficult to deal with. Once the racer enters eastern Colorado, then Kansas, the scenery is unrelentingly similar. In addition, night riding, even in the headlights of the follow vehicle, is like riding in a tunnel with a fog line on the right and a lane line on the left. The universe shrinks down to a small stretch of the road. For the Honey Badger, training in central Illinois was very helpful. Thousands of miles of tar roads go through corn fields, accompanied by relentless 10-15 mile per hour winds, ridden as head winds half of the time. Riding the same straight roads produced a state of familiarity that translated during the race into a sense of equanimity. The Honey Badger greeted the flat segments as a reminder of home. We strongly recommend getting experience dealing with the same monotonous terrain over and over while riding alone, as well as riding at night over and over again. It gives the race a familiarity that fortifies the racer against the boredom, instead of compounding it. The Honey Badger never had a temper tantrum, never threw his bike around, and never complained to the crew that he would quit during the race. He just pushed the pedals about a million times, listened to music and GPS audio cues, was fed and put to bed by the crews, and all of a sudden he was at the finish line.

The racer's entertainment is a key factor in dealing with monotony. This will be very idiosyncratic. The Honey Badger found a combination of classical, jazz and rock music, interspersed occasionally with an audio book chapter, to be very helpful. This played along with the GPS cues from RideWithGPS through the single earbud allowed by RAAM management. It keeps you awake during the lonely and quiet night hours, which constitute half of this strategy's race time. Make sure there are no annoying songs among the lot. You may think that it will help keep you on edge, but on Day 9 of RAAM, annoying stuff is just ... annoying. The Honey Badger listened to all his songs 100s of times for months ahead of the race, so there was no surprise. They were all like welcome friends that would visit in random order thanks to shuffling, but welcome nonetheless. Martin used music and pieces of audiobooks for the first 10 days, abandoning them for the outside world only on the morning of

Day 11 as he was approaching Annapolis. Others may need a different entertainment strategy: Perhaps nothing at all except for the occasional GPS cue; or perhaps an unknown playlist put together by a friend, full of surprises. Or perhaps the canonical RAAM approach of loudspeakers blaring from the crew vehicle into the night. Whatever it is, racers must make sure that on their longer 500- to 1500-mile practice races, it leaves them very happy. Anything short of very happy over 500 miles turns into very sour over 3000 miles.

Training at Night

Point 2 of our race strategy in Chapter 2 bears repeating:

> "2. It is imperative that the hottest hours of the day, generally noon to 16:00, be avoided in favor of night riding. The dehydration and heat stress during the mid-day hours take the greatest toll on the racer."

Extensive training at night, by logging thousands of miles a year at night, was important for dealing with night riding safely while maintaining high speeds, but it was even more important to get the rider used to the quiet tunnel effect that prevails at night. The Honey Badger greeted each night for its cooler temperatures, instead of being afraid of lower visibility or monotony.

Many racers who do just fine during the day, are worried about the night:

- You are less visible, and could get hit by a car or truck.
- Your vision is not as acute, and with less illumination, you may miss potholes, gravel patches and other obstacles in the road.
- Speedy descents are more dangerous, particularly in the rain.
- You are more prone to falling asleep on the bike.
- You can't see the scenery, so it is even more monotonous than during the day.

Well, yes and no. Many of these fears are actually unfounded, and can be overcome by regular night training.

During the race, your follow vehicle will do just that every night: follow about 20-30 feet behind you. You will not see the road in the beam of a bicycle headlamp with limited output power, but instead in the much brighter headlights, even the brights (when there's low traffic) of your crew vehicle. If you train alone at night (pick quiet roads and have proper illumination!), then by comparison the follow vehicle will seem like a great source of brightness during RAAM. You want to make sure you optimize positioning of any extra lights on your crew vehicle: the Honey Badger didn't care, but some racers don't like the shadows they cast in the lights of their follow vehicle.

Regarding visibility, the issue is not whether you are visible, but whether the rear of your follow vehicle is visible to traffic behind you. There is a reason flashing lights are race-mandatory on the crew vehicle. A good example is Highway 50 in West Virginia, which the Honey Badger rode during the day in 2013 and at night in 2016. The latter felt much safer because 18-wheeler traffic was at a minimum at night, and the follow vehicle with its flashing lights and glowing rear triangle was visible from afar. During the day, Highway 50 was indeed fearsome, with numerous honking 18-wheelers passing every minute, forcing us deep onto the debris-strewn shoulder. Reviewing past records of severe accidents and even deaths during RAAM, they are more likely to occur during the day than during the night. Likewise, crew vehicles are not known to frequently run over their own racers due to crew fatigue, and if you follow the crew **keystones 4** and **5**, it is even less likely that one of your three crews will get dangerously tired.

Your vision is certainly less acute at night, but you have your vehicle's illumination. Wear yellow lenses, which enhance contrast very advantageously. If your night vision is naturally not very good, consider adding extra headlights to your follow vehicles, to provide even stronger illumination. They may have to be turned down (as do the brights) when there is oncoming traffic, but some of the darkest and most desolate stretches at night (e.g. in the desert) have very low traffic, and you will be able to make good use of the extra illumination.

Descents are more dangerous in the dark, especially in the rain, snow (on Wolf Creek Pass), or fog (Appalachians), but there is really a simple countermeasure: just don't descend as fast. This may seem obvious, but many racers feel regrets descending at 15-20 mph while feathering their brakes, when they could do an easy 40 mph. After all, it's 'free' time and precious climbing power wasted. However, the gain in safety during low visibility periods (night, fog, etc.) is worth it. Case in point: in 2013, the Honey Badger's teammate really pushed the descents in Brown County, Indiana, until he wiped out on some gravel, breaking his bike and nearly ending the race for himself. In contrast, the Honey Badger went downhill well within his handling ability, especially during rainy nights. One time, he even waited in the car during a particularly bad nighttime storm in Ohio. Yes, a total of about an hour and a half was probably lost during the race in 2016 due to slower riding or waiting in the dark, but imagine the alternatives: crashing by descending too fast; or baking in the desert sun for 12+ hours a day without a 4 hour break.

The 'falling asleep on the bike at night' issue is a non-issue, as long as you have properly prepared for our strategy by *jet-lagging yourself so your normal sleep cycle is from 4 AM to 11 AM California time at the start of the race*. While other racers will begin to feel very sleepy around 4 AM, for you it's still 'early evening' in your personal jet-lagged time zone, and you will have no problem riding through the night until the sun rises again and makes it easier to stay awake. As discussed elsewhere in this book, the proper caffeine dose administered in the early morning hours can also help here. The Honey Badger never felt sleepy at night. Indeed, the one time he nodded off was during the late morning hours, when he had not slept well the day before (see Figure 3.14, day 5.5 data).

The last bullet point listed above is a real problem. Night riding is like riding in a tunnel between fog line and center line, and the monotony is much greater than during the day. This is where extensive night training, with the entertainment of your choice, becomes important. Remember that you will need to ride at night anyway. Even if you sleep several hours at night, it will still be dark for 5+ hours, so there is no escaping night riding during RAAM if you want to finish within the tough time limit. Thus, embrace night riding, practice it, and it will become your cool friend, not your feared foe.

Desert Heat and Altitude

Even if you ride all night and sleep in the middle of the day, you will still encounter dry heat (110 °F, 20% humidity) in the desert, and humid heat (90 °F, 50% humidity) in the Midwest. We will not go at length into the necessary preparation, but mention a few points:

- Losing some body fat can help thermoregulation. Even a race like RAAM does not require immense body fat resources to be completed in 8-12 days. The 180 cm (5'11") Honey Badger typically leans down by about 2 kg (4.5 lb.) before major races (from 65 to 63 kg).
- Dry heat training, such as sitting in a sauna for up to 2 hours/day, two to three weeks before the race, may be helpful. It is recommended for ultrarunners doing extreme desert races such as Badwater.
- Make sure on your training rides to get used to consuming large quantities of fluid with calories (see "feeding schedule" in Chapter 8). Starving yourself of fluids and nutrition will not help – don't treat your training rides as weight-loss opportunities.

Likewise, altitude sickness can be a problem for some racers. Some of the passes to be crossed are above 10,000 feet (3000 m). Unfortunately, altitude training is not an option for everyone, and like heat acclimatization, it takes at least 2 weeks to show some results. If you can afford it, do it. Otherwise your best options are:

- Do not unnecessarily rev up your heart rate in the mountains. It easily happens at altitude while you feel 'good,' but has a price later in the race.
- Extend your sleep breaks before high-altitude sections (add 0.5 to 1 hour). This is also a good idea before the desert heat. You can shorten your sleep breaks during the second half of the race.

Many racers make the mistake in particular of cutting out the sleep cycle after day 1, when you are likely to be doing some hot climbing (e.g. up Yarnell pass). We know you still feel pretty fresh after day 1, but resist the temptation of cutting out your first sleep break. Unnecessary fatigue is cumulative.

Think about Strategic Support During the Race

A related mental element is support during the race. Most important, and always there, is of course the crew. The racer needs to be honest with them regarding the kind of encouragement that is helpful, and the kind that is annoying. For example, ringing a cowbell to get Martin to drink, or telling him he just passed the Tour de France distance worked; getting him to solve a riddle while riding did not work. The crew will be happy to do what it takes to keep their racer awake, motivated, and moving forward. Also important are cheering friends and family along the route, if it can be arranged. The Honey Badger sent out an email to friends across the US who lived not too far from the route, in places like Jerome, AZ, Greensburg, IN, or Mt. Airy, MD, all along the route. Not everyone could make it, but about 40 people showed up at various places along the entire route to cheer on the racer. These were nice boosts, and a visit by Illinois friends and family left Martin with a lump in his throat. Getting friends and family to the race can be an expensive undertaking if you are based in Europe or elsewhere outside the US, but having friends and family share in the race is uplifting for them and the racer alike, and worth the extra cost.

Know Your Competition, but Don't Follow Their Every Move

Another mental element is knowing the competition. All RAAM racers went through a qualification process and are well-trained. In 2016, the Honey Badger (a RAAM rookie with racer number #564) was up against a number of RAAM veterans and strong ultracyclists from around the world. #480 (Palle Nielsen from Denmark) had placed 2nd twice at the Borrego Springs World 24 Hour Worlds TT, and raced solo RAAM in 2013, while #564 raced two-man team RAAM. #492 (Chris O'Keefe from the US) finished RAW in just over 3 days in 2012. It is noteworthy that all three Masters podium finishers reached the RAW finish line (TS 15 in Durango) between 2d 21h and 3d 4h in 2016, without exception before the RAW solo Masters winner of 2016 (see Table 5.2). Thus all three were better trained than the fastest RAW solo Masters competitors. This is not unusual if one checks the statistics over many years of RAW and RAAM.

Table 5.2. The TS #15 Durango times for the 2016 RAAM Masters male riders on the final podium *vs.* the Masters and Open male podiums of RAW. The overall RAW winner was Sarah Cooper in 2d 11h 59m. Sarah Cooper also won the Open Female division of RAAM in 2017.

Final podium	RAAM Masters	RAW Masters	RAW Open Male
1	2 d 23 h 29 m	3 d 03 h 58 m	2 d 14 h 09 m
2	3 d 03 h 42 m	3 d 19 h 05 m	2 d 16 h 25 m
3	2 d 21 h 12 m	3 d 20 h 17 m	2 d 16 h 38 m

The 2016 RAAM Masters podium does not conclude the list of strong racers. Franco Micolini (#524) of the Italian Team Super Heroes, placed 3rd in the very tough Swiss cycling Marathon in 2014, and went to TS 41 in 9 days in 2015 in solo RAAM. Martin Bergmeister (#559, also a 2016 rookie) from Team Brixen of South Tyrol, Italy, won the Race Across Italy Masters title and the Ultracycling Italian Championship Masters title in 2015. Morten Kjaesgaard (#448), also from Denmark, had participated in RAAM in 2012 and 2014. Two of them also beat the RAW Masters Champion of 2016 to Durango, and the third came close. These six racers had the aerobic capacity and training to race a 10 day solo RAAM under optimal weather conditions, or in 11 days under less than optimal conditions, and so did several others who had to DNF for various reasons.

Thus, race strategy was going to be the major determining factor in 2016, not any super-strong rider just riding away from the pack. Winning the Masters division of RAAM was a question of the optimal timing and duration of sleep periods that would provide the best compromise between time lost sleeping and time lost slowing down due to fatigue. This knowledge only cemented our determination to implement the optimal sleep schedule, even if it would put us behind during the first phase of the race. One can see this by looking at the first 100 hours of Figure 3.7 in Chapter 3.

Two final important elements of racer preparation are tapering and the crew practice race, listed in Table 4.1 in March 2016. Tapering is discussed in Chapter 8. The crew training race will be discussed in detail in the next chapter, which covers the RAAM crew. The practice race serves both to calibrate the racer on crew behavior, and to get the crew up to speed. Before the practice race, which was held on part of the 2016 RAAM course, Martin participated in a two-day, 262-mile training camp of his cycling club, the Wild Cards. The practice race with crew was about 350 miles in two segments, bringing the total 4-day training mileage to about 600 miles.

To summarize the message of Chapter 5: Put in a cumulative 1500 mile race effort every year for three years before solo RAAM. Skip the sleep-deprived 24-hour races that ruin your training capacity. Instead do many 12-hour events, as well as 500- to 900-mile events with proper sleep breaks (2-4 hours every 20 to 22 hours) in the three years before solo RAAM (**keystone 1** of our race strategy). Keep an eye on your HR=180-age for training, and expect HR=160-age as the 10+ day average feasible during the race. Mix in some interval training, and don't feel bad if half of your training is slow and just burns fat, you still can use it to test sleep breaks, learn to ride at night, and gain saddle time (**keystones 1 to 3** of our strategy). Make sure you calibrate the duration of your sleep break, it should be about 2 REM cycles + nod-off time for a Masters racer, less for a younger racer. Use your speed at HR = 160 - age to make time estimates for your race (Chapter 8). Use your training and your races to focus on maintaining a feasible heart rate with iron discipline. A controlled heart rate will serve you well in the first 3 to 4 days of solo RAAM, when many competitors ride too hard, and burn matches they need on days 7 through 10. Spend years finding the right saddles, shorts, and shoes, and rotate through them to vary pressure points. Optimize your entertainment during the race by making sure it left you very happy during a 500- to 1500-mile race. Ride at night, night, night and make sure you are satisfied with the illumination provided by your crew vehicles. Study the competition, but don't let your crew tell you where you stand until 3 days before the end of the race. Race your own race without outside interference until you cross the Mississippi. The Big River is where many RAAM veterans feel the race really starts, and rightly so.

6. PRE-RACE **PREPARATION** – THE CREW

The racer preparation outlined in Chapter 5 is important, but nothing, absolutely nothing, is more important for solo RAAM success than a good crew. A functional crew makes the race. A dysfunctional crew breaks the race. This chapter discusses crew selection and crew training for the "long sleep-long ride" strategy espoused by this book. Our approach requires a crew comprised of three sub-crews, optimized to avoid conflict, provide short shifts, good rest and allow for redundancy should one of the sub-crews fail. We remind the reader of **keystones 4 and 5** for an optimal crew experience:

4. Make use of only 2 stationary crew exchanges for racer hygiene breaks.
5. Two crew members in each of three vehicles keeps the crews busy, yet rested with roughly 6-7 hour shifts.

Crews are obligatory during RAAM for many reasons. They protect the back of the racer on busy roads, like the frightening US 50 in West Virginia. They provide regular food and drink during uninterrupted 19+ hour rides during the race, via stationary hand-offs (in leapfrog mode) or window hand-offs (in follow mode). They solve unexpected problems, from wheels that do not fit between brakes to a racer's sudden craving for pizza. And most importantly, they provide constant encouragement and emotional boosts, often verbally, but even more so simply by being there. What racer has not nearly despaired during a tough segment of RAAM, and thought "I can't let my crew down. They are sacrificing weeks of their lives for me, they're driving right behind me right now, and I'm thinking of quitting?" That thought alone always got the Honey Badger to put a smile back on his face and start pedaling harder.

Our recommended crew strategy is predicated on two simple points.

1. The crew must be kept **very busy**, yet must remain reasonably **well-rested** throughout the race.

2. There must be enough **redundancy** to cope with the unexpected, and enough **expertise** to cope with the expected.

To make a long story short, (1) requires that there be three follow crews (to be well-rested by doing only 7 hour shifts), but that each of the three follow vehicles have only 2 crew members (to keep each crew member very busy and reduce the chance of idle conflict). (2) requires that the crew be made up people with varied skill sets such as bicycle maintenance and repair, computer skills, first aid and experience in endurance sports, as well as personalities that foster a spirit of cooperation and flexibility in potentially difficult situations. It also requires backup crew along the route.

During the 2013 two-man team RAAM, the Honey Badger had three people per vehicle on his crew, a common choice among RAAM racers. It provides some redundancy in case someone gets sick or bows out, and divides up driving/navigating/feeding tasks more easily during the race. However, it became amply clear during the race that three people were not fully busy in this day and age of GPS automation and sophisticated scheduling. As a result, idle strife developed as the days wore on. Thus we are convinced that two crew members per vehicle is a superior choice, and this was fully borne out during the 2016 race. It is much easier to find two people who click well than to find three. Moreover, they will be much busier, leaving no time for idle thoughts, overestimating one's own abilities, or underestimating others' abilities. Instead, it is better to provide redundancy by having three follow vehicles instead of two, and by having backup crew members along the route, who are ready to jump in during the race when needed. This is exactly what we did, and it worked very well in 2016.

When there are two crew members in a follow vehicle, the roles split into driver, and navigator/feeder. The latter job is often done by two people, but one works better. Even in the busiest segments of RAAM, the direction changes are not that frequent, and modern technology has changed the navigator job completely. The racer gunning for a top finish should be equipped with an earbud and GPS voice cues throughout the race (Chapter 7), eliminating the need for the navigator to constantly direct the racer through blaring megaphones. The Honey Badger had no loudspeakers of any kind on his crew vehicles. Likewise, the same GPS software makes it easy for the navigator to direct the driver, although the route book still plays a key role (Chapter 9).

Three crews and three follow vehicles are needed to split the average 19.5-hour daily ride time into three 6- to 7-hour shifts rather than two nearly 10-hour shifts. Driving slowly behind a racer for up to 7 hours is hard enough, let alone 10 hours. The winning strategy discussed here involves a lot of riding between 19:00 and 09:00, when follow mode is obligatory during RAAM. So the crews have to do a lot of slow following.

In addition, three crews provide the redundancy previously sought with three members per crew. If one of the crews has an accident, or for other reasons ceases to function either temporarily or permanently, the active crew simply continues 3 hours longer, and the remaining off-duty crew gets started 3 hours earlier. The resulting 10 hour shifts (both crews are off during the 4 hour sleep) are more stressful, but can be handled for a few days by two crews, or until the third crew is back in action. Of course the latter may not happen at all. That is why it is important to have backup volunteers along the course, who can hop in with one of the remaining crews. Or hop in even if all three crews are active: the backup can replace a crew member, or enlarge a crew to 3 with a fresh member late in the race, when strife has less time to build up.

Even with three crews of two, 7 hours on and 17 hours off is much harder than it seems. The crews have to drive forward about 200 miles each day on their own in order to keep up with a racer covering 300 miles a day. Most of that driving is on the race course, often too far away from interstate freeways to allow shortcuts. That means speeds around 40-50 mph for the crew, or up to 5 hours of driving. The crews should get at least 7 hours of sleep to be well rested, in good spirits, and safe drivers behind their racer. That totals up to 7+5+7=19 hours so far. The remaining 5 hours of the day will not be idle, as the crew purchases food and sundry items for themselves or for the racer, makes hotel reservations, maintains bikes, tanks up vehicles, confers with other crews (about the next day's racing, weather forecasts, unforeseen problems, and the competition), or does a little bit of sight-seeing along the route. All of this could probably just barely get done by two crews with 10-hour shifts, but the slightest problem would stress them over the limit. So three follow vehicles is a good compromise between cost and crew fatigue.

The Honey Badger found six reliable people as potential crew, plus several more to step-in 'fresh' along the route if needed. One of them actually did step in during the race, in Effingham, to help out as a fresh driver for a very tired crew #3. The crews were divided into three 6.5-hour shifts, nominally from 16:30 to 23:30 (racer wake-up crew, or Crew #1), 23:30 to 06:00 (the night shift, or Crew #2), and 06:00 to 12:30 (the racer bedtime crew, or Crew #3). Their specialized tasks and interactions during the actual RAAM are described in much more detail in Chapter 9 and in the race chronology in Chapter 12. In this chapter the focus is on crew selection and pre-race training.

The initial solo RAAM crew members were chosen by contacting people the racer was familiar with, and empowering them to find their own crew mate. The Honey Badger's first contact was Harry Zink, who had been the racer's crew chief during the 2013 two-man team RAAM race. He was a natural choice because he had RAAM crewing experience, and was able to make himself available again in 2016. Another initial contact was Julie Turner, a school teacher with summer availability who does a lot of riding, and whose husband, Jeff Turner, is also an ultracyclist. She engaged her niece Lana Pohlmann from Florida, to make it a "women's road adventure." The two got along well, and knew each other from annual family gatherings, but had never worked together so closely for so long. RAAM was a welcome chance for friendship and bonding. Both agreed afterwards that RAAM was very beneficial to them in that regard, and it is a big plus if the crew, not just the racer, can get something out of the race beyond the sum of the parts. The last initial contact was Greg Scott, a runner and triathlete, whom Martin knew well because he had been Greg's PhD advisor before Greg took on a professorship at Cal Poly San Luis Obispo. Greg engaged his father Ed Scott, who has a medical degree. They treated this as a "father-son road trip" and also spent far more time together than usual, to good effect. Finally, The Honey Badger had to find a second crew member for Harry Zink, and advertised the position at a large group ride of the Prairie Cycle Club, a local riding club in the Champaign-Urbana area. Roy Tylinksi, a former Illinois student and now barista, was immediately interested, and eventually signed on to crew with Harry Zink. Roy and Harry were the only two crew who did not know each other well, and for them, the practice race discussed further below would be an important testing ground to make sure the crew chemistry was right in all three vehicles.

Thus the crews ended up as follows:

Crew #1: Julie Turner and Lana Pohlmann, relatives who used to the race as a road adventure and aunt-niece friendship opportunity. They made up the evening crew, in charge of prepping the racer's kit, waking up the racer, breakfast, and taking the racer on his first 6 to 7 hours of riding after the rest period. They crewed late afternoon and evening from about 16:00 to about 23:00 during the race, as discussed in Chapters 2 and 8. Julie was our expert in nutrition, food preparation for the racer as well as crew. Lana was a master navigator and kept the organizational flow of the crew smooth as well as the racer supplied without a fault.

Crew #2: Harry Zink and Roy Tylinski made up the night crew, roughly from 23:00 to 05:30. Harry was crew chief, and in charge of the racer's sleep decisions and hygiene reminders. More than once he decreed extra sleep or shorter ride days during the race, which proved beneficial in the long run. Roy was the bike wrangling expert, able to repair bikes on the fly while on the backseat of a driving vehicle and simultaneously feeding the racer, when Harry was driving. This proved to be a very useful skill as there were plenty of small technical problems with the bikes.

Crew #2, Julie Turner (left) and Lana Pohlmann (right), are taking a power nap while waiting for the racer to wake up. Crews #1 and #3 had plenty of sleep during the race, but Crew #2 needed driving help about three quarters of the way through the race because they did not adapt fully to daytime sleep before the race.

Crew #3: Greg and Ed Scott functioned throughout the race as the morning crew, putting the racer to bed at a motel or in the back of their van on a sleeping pad, typically around noon after a 05:30 to 12:00 shift. They had the important task of keeping the racer on a good sleep schedule, securing a motel for the racer each day, yet making sure the maximum possible mileage was covered without messing up the sleep schedule. Greg is a logistics expert, familiar with caffeine dosing for endurance and able to do accurate predictions of race distances and times throughout the race. Ed checked in with the racer about minor aches and pains, and consulted with an ophthalmologist about eye drops to help with Martin's red eye.

Several other crew members were held in reserve, near Jerome, AZ and Effingham, IL. As it turned out, the night crew did not fully adapt to their "sleep during the day, drive at night" cycle before the race (they have jobs!), and got quite tired by Day 7. Thus we brought in Jay Yost as a fresh third crew member for the night shift. He joined Crew #2 in Effingham, and did much of their driving for the last 700 miles. Jay is a two-man team RAAM veteran racer, and also an experienced crew member for other RAAM racers, so he immediately settled into the routine. Jay knew both Harry and Roy, either from a previous two-person RAAM, or from club rides at home. The other two crews had regular night sleep, and did not require a third crew member later in the race.

With the exception of Harry Zink and Jay Yost, none of the crew had prior experience with RAAM, although several had a good understanding of endurance sports and cycling. Moreover, two crew members had never met one another. Thus it was important to conduct a practice race, which was held in March 2016, about 3 months before the actual solo RAAM effort.

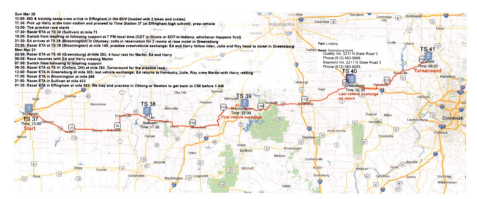

Figure 6.1 The RAAM practice race. The Honey Badger and two crew members are based out of Champaign-Urbana in Illinois. Thus the practice race was held from time stations 37 to 41 on the RAAM route, which provides a typical measure of flat (in Illinois) and hilly terrain (in Brown County). The racer started at noon and progressed from TS 37 to TS 40 before resting, then to TS 41 and part of the way back to TS 38. That regimen simulated about half a RAAM day, followed by a rest, followed by another half RAAM day.

Before the practice race, Martin participated in a two-day, 262-mile training camp held by his cycling club, the Wild Cards. The practice race was about another 350 miles in two segments separated by a short sleep cycle. No one had jet-lagged for the practice race, so the sleep cycle was held at about 2 AM in the early morning hours, rather than at noon during the day. The map in Figure 6.1 shows the trajectory of the practice race, which took the crew to 5 time stations from Illinois to Ohio.

Present were Harry, Julie, Roy, and Ed, so at least one representative from each crew vehicle was there to be trained. We went through multiple crew exchanges with two vehicles, especially stationary exchanges that were going to be important during the race, but also moving exchanges in case the need should arise. The crew got drilled in bed time and awakening procedures at the hotel in Greenburg, Indiana (Chapter 9). They practiced vehicle hand-offs during follow mode, as well as stationary handoffs during daytime leapfrog mode, and waving directions for the racer. The latter was rarely necessary during the race because the Honey Badger had a GPS device with map and voice directions, which was also tested during the practice race. However, there were a few re-routes due to storm damage and construction during the actual race, where directions from the crew proved useful. The route book from RAAM 2013 was along, and the crew got basic instruction on the route book. After two days of training, the crew had a solid idea of the various tasks that needed to be performed. Much of this would be repeated again during two days before the race in Oceanside, as a refresher course for the "veterans," as well as training for the crew members who had not participated in the practice race.

By the end of the practice race, it was very clear that Harry and Roy had a good rapport, and would work well together. This took care of the last doubts the racer had about the crew several months before the actual race. It should be obvious that having the crew work together extensively before the race is a good idea, but we confess that this did not happen before the 2013 two-man race on the Honey Badger's crew, with all kinds of difficulties ensuing during the race. So the main lesson here is: even if it costs you $1000+ to have a multi-day practice race on the actual course with as many of your crew present as possible, it is worth every bit you spend on it. If you live in Europe or Asia and can't afford an extra trip to the US, nevertheless do a practice race near home, on terrain that includes a lot of climbing, and that you can ride at night. Do not cobble together a crew that meet each other in Oceanside for the first time – it can be a recipe for disaster.

7. PRE-RACE PREPARATION – EQUIPMENT **AND** SUPPLIES

A long race like RAAM has many contingencies, and so the three crew vehicles must have plenty of equipment and supplies on board. Here, we concentrate on equipment not likely to change much over the years – that is, *not* the latest electronic GPS or power-tracking gadget. The key points for preparing equipment and supplies were as follows.

Rental vehicles. We decided to operate with three insured rental vehicles as follow vehicles to reduce hassles from vehicle malfunctions or accidents as much as possible. Of the vehicles we tested, the Dodge Caravan was by far the best. Despite its relatively small exterior size, it offered a lot of interior space for up to three people (in case the racer needed ferrying or a third crew member joined), easy storage of two bicycles and the supply crates, as well as a convenient sliding door for rear seat access by a tired racer. We also used Ford Expeditions, but found this SUV less desirable. Although larger optically from the outside (see Photo 7.1), it had a harder time accommodating 2 bicycles and 3 people, the middle row of seats did not fold down as nicely as in the Caravan, and the lack of a sliding door made entry of the tired racer for hygiene sessions during crew exchanges more difficult. The lesson here is that it is worth testing vehicles during the practice race or the two-man team RAAM, and insist on the best fit. In our case, the rental agency was unable to make the requested vehicle type available on the rental day, and an Expedition was used as a substitute. We rented only 1 day ahead of our drive to Oceanside. One way to alleviate this problem is to rent two days ahead and insist on delivery of the exact vehicle requested.

Photo 7.1. Mounting of rear amber flash lights and magnetic rear triangles during inspection. All bikes were carried inside the vehicles, for better visibility and aerodynamics. The race helmets and shoes are laid out next to the black SUV driven by Crew #3.

All the vans we used had three rows of seats. The last row was folded into the floor to make room for internal transport of all bicycles. In the second row, the seat behind the driver was folded into the floor, and the cooler was placed there. The water jugs, a milk crate containing food, and another milk crate containing clothing were placed in the middle (front to back), so the jugs and food were easily accessible to the navigator/feeder. The right seat of the middle row was left up, so another crew member or the racer could use it if the situation demanded it (*e.g.* RAAM-enforced ferrying of the racer through construction). That seat was also used as a platform by the racer for the hygiene bag, and any clothes taken from the clothes crate during crew exchanges (see Figure 9.1 in Chapter 9).

The vehicles we used all had 12 V outlets in the middle and back of the van, in addition to the driver's area. The rear plugs were used for the amber roof mounted flashlights (see Photo 7.1). The flashlights were taped off at the front with duct tape, and taped to the rear roof of the vehicles with duct tape. Finally, they were plugged into the 12 V outlet in the back or middle, to avoid cables criss-crossing at the front of the vehicle.

Two ways of mounting the slow vehicle triangles were used. All triangles were equipped with a pair of strong neodymium magnets, screwed to the triangle with wing nuts. The van on the right in Photo 7.1 (a Grand Caravan minivan, the preferred vehicle) had a metal hatch, and the triangle was simply clicked onto the hatch like a refrigerator magnet. The SUV on the left had a plastic hatch, which would not hold a magnetic triangle. A steel tow bar was installed, and the triangle was clicked to it. Both triangles could be pulled off and clicked on in seconds.

Photo 7.2. The four bicycles used in the race.

Bicycles. We decided to bring along four bicycles, three to be ridden at regular intervals during the race (Chapter 8), and one additional bike for contingencies. Thus, the crew vans usually each carried one bike while the racer was on the fourth, although a van occasionally carried two bikes to ferry a bike to the next crew. With proper planning, the racer ended up with the two optimal bike choices at all times during the race (Chapter 7). The bicycles are shown in Photo 7.2. The Giant TCR0 is equipped with a regular road handle bar and aerobars, a configuration suitable for almost any combination of flat terrain and climbing. The Merlin titanium bike with only a road handlebar was lightweight and specialized for steep long climbs. The Superbike (with a Dimond frame handmade in Des Moines, Iowa by Rüster Sports) was by far the fastest time trial bike, outperforming the already very good CTT (carbon time trial) bike by about 0.5 mph at the same heart rate and wind conditions. It was the first choice for the middle 800 miles of the race from eastern Colorado through Illinois, as well as flat sections in California and Arizona. The Superbike is an aerodynamically designed beam bike, and also offered better riding comfort than the TCR0 or CTT in the aero position. Compared to the CTT bike, the Superbike uses a relatively un-aggressive aero position (3" drop from saddle to aerobar pad), and a slightly longer 0.885xInseam bottom bracket to top-of-saddle distance to account for very slight flexing of the beam. The CTT bike, our back-up in case of major mechanical problems with another bike, was never actually used during the 2016 race. Each bicycle was equipped to be autonomous. It had its own headlights, tail light, and two bento boxes, one for equipment and one for food and cable stowage (Photo 6.3).

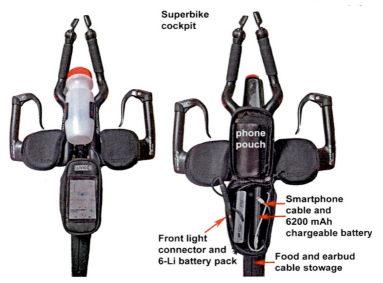

Photo 7.3. The superbike cockpit illustrates the two bento boxes. The top bento box (DUUTI) houses the smartphone battery and front light battery. The front light cable is fed into the bento through a hand-cut hole. The earbud audio cord (not shown) is also fed through a hole. Its cable and earbud can be stowed in the lower slotted bento box (Torhans) along with gels or energy bars.

Cockpit configuration. The equipment bento box housed a 6 Li-cell battery pack that could run the headlight for 18 hours before battery pack exchange (Photo 7.4). This battery pack was only exchanged when the light went out. The equipment bento box also housed the smartphone that provided RideWithGPS audio cues/directions, music/audio entertainment, and a real-time map, speed and heart rate information. The bento box had a clear plastic window for the smartphone, which was easily inserted in the phone pouch. Finally, the equipment bento box housed the smartphone battery and its USB-to-phone cable. During stationary crew exchanges, the previous crew would recover its smartphone battery for charging, and the new crew would hook their freshly charged battery up to the smartphone while the racer was doing hygiene.

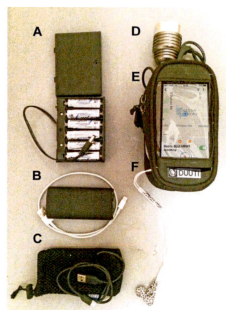

Photo 7.4. The cockpit equipment used. It was identical on each bike, so crews could quickly swap the front light battery (A) case every 18 hours, and the smartphone battery (B) every 6 to 7 hours during crew exchange. (C) shows the smartphone battery pouch and charger cable kept in the crew vehicle, (D) the front LED light, (E) the equipment bento box with the smartphone running RideWithGPS, and (F) the earbuds. Only one earbud is allowed in the right ear during the race per RAAM rules, and piped voice GPS directions as well as music and audio books to the racer. The light was a generic CREE LED purchased for $17, and all 5 (including a spare) performed flawlessly during P-B-P and RAAM. Its rechargeable battery was replaced by a 6 x 1.5 V case (A) from Uxcell, supplemented by a 2.1 x 5.5 mm DC female-to-female coupler to provide the necessary 9 V to the headlight. Note that if you use a case such as (A), it is imperative that you epoxy the battery contact springs to the case. They will otherwise pop out when the crew pulls used batteries, rendering the case inoperable.

Important: you must set the smartphone light level to maximum unless you want to rely just on audio cues. Otherwise the display will be impossible to read during the daylight. In addition, most smartphones cannot handle temperatures above 110 °F, or direct exposure to the heat of the sun even at lower temperatures. During some daytime operation, this required the phone and its battery to be carried in the racer's left back pocket. The exchange was effected in a few seconds during a Nature break or other short stop. As a backup for reading the heart rate, it is useful to also wear a simple wrist heart rate monitor that displays instantaneous and average heart rate. Smart watches are getting better every year, and can provide heartrate info and even visual directional cues from the Bluetooth-tethered smartphone. We did not use a smartwatch in 2016 because the available audio cue capabilities were still quite rudimentary compared to RideWithGPS on a smartphone. We also don't recommend sports watches with proprietary (non-Bluetooth) connectivity.

The racer decided early on after testing some Bluetooth headsets that the frequent battery changes, as well as pairing idiosyncrasies, would cause more delay than the wireless connectivity was worth, and opted for an ordinary mini-jack earbud. This will change in the future, as low-power Bluetooth gets ever more reliable and is likely to exceed 8 hours of battery life, allowing headsets to be swapped at crew exchanges. Until then, the earbud provides continuous directional cues from the RideWithGPS app running on the smartphone in the bento box, and is easily unplugged and re-plugged during nature breaks. But beware, and bring a spare: the Honey Badger once forgot to plug it back in, and ripped the earbud wire to shreds in his front wheel.

In the future, satellite GPS transceivers are likely to take over. Already in 2016, RAAM management had racers carry a small satellite GPS transceiver, and as the technology improves and becomes fully personalized, satellite/wireless solutions with a battery lifetime that lasts throughout the whole of RAAM will become a reality. This will greatly simplify the crew's ability to track their racer's position and heart rate.

The second bento box was used to store food items, or stow the earbud cable, and was mounted behind the equipment bento box. It was either a slotted type (Torhans, see Photo 7.3), into which bars and gels could simply be stuck, or a net-covered type (Bontrager). Other designs with zippers or rain covers were found not to work easily during long rides, and were abandoned during the racer training phase.

Photo 7.5. The black clothing and supplies crate (left) with a RAAM jersey, and the red special clothes crate, with the yellow O2 rain jacket on top (right). In addition, some contents of the black food crate (not shown) are shown on the left, as well as some contents of the red special supplies and tools crate (not shown). Each van also had a spare front and rear wheel, a slow vehicle triangle and amber flash lights, in addition to other items not shown. Each crew member was supplied with a technical T-shirt and a hooded sweatshirt bearing the team logo.

Supply and equipment crates. Each of the three follow vehicles was equipped with its own two black milk crates, each with identical contents (Photo 7.5). In addition, there were two red milk crates that contained more specialized items that were moved from one crew to the next at each stationary crew exchange. The color coding of crates made the move straightforward (Chapter 9). Only the two red crates and the racer's hygiene/rest backpack, and sometimes a bicycle, had to be moved during two crew exchanges. (The third exchange was at a motel with the racer resting, and had no time constraints.)

Black crate #1 carried the most essential food and medical supplies that the navigator/feeder would have to use during follow mode or leapfrog mode. Black crate #2 contained the crew's main supply of racer clothes, used at wake-up or crew exchanges as needed. It also held the crew's smartphone battery, and most frequently needed supplies. Red crate #1 contained special clothing for very cold weather (one of the mountain descents at night), rain storms (the racer encountered two in 2016), or cooler nights (many), as well as spare kit and shoes. Red crate #2 stored tools and many spare parts. In addition, each individual vehicle was supplied with a medical kit, cooler, crew reflective vests and ankle bands, slow vehicle triangles, amber flashlights, bicycle pumps, and other items listed below. The table below lists the inventory of each type of crate and for the vehicles. Almost all the items listed there found use at one time or another during the race. The crew purchased various other items en route. Some of these have been added to the inventory after the fact because they turned out to be so useful that they should have been included from the beginning.

Crate and vehicle inventories

Black crate #1 (food and medical), duplicated in each follow vehicle
1	Large bucket of HEED/Gatorade 50:50 premix (use 1 large scoop per bottle)
3	Bike bottles
22	Assorted energy bars (2+ per shift)
1	Gel plastic container, holds 5 servings (2+ per shift)
1	Bottle of gel
1	Bottle electrolyte pills (1 per hour during the daytime)
1	Sunscreen spray, SPF50 or SPF 70
1	Medicated numbing spray (Lanacane)
2	Plastic bags

Black crate #2 (clothing and supplies), duplicated in each follow vehicle
1	Bib short
1	Jersey
1	Pair of socks
1	Long-sleeved thermal upper
1	Tool supply bag, containing: spare tube, multi-tool, tire levers, box cutter, tire boot
1	Smartphone battery (Anker 6200 mAh) and charging cable
1	Duct tape
1	Flashlight
1	Package of degreasing wipes
1	Toilet paper roll
1	Plastic bag (for soiled shorts and clothing)

Red crate #1 (special clothing), exchanged during crew exchange

2	Extra pairs of shorts, jerseys, socks
1	Night helmet (more aerodynamic, less vented)
1	Extra pair of reflective-labeled bike shoes
1	Rain supply bag (contains rain gloves, O2 rain jacket, helmet cover)
1	Rain supply bag (contains O2 long rain pants, rain shorts)
1	Wind jacket, Honey badger logo
1	Heavy jacket (e.g. Gore-Tex winter jacket) and heavy gloves (for <40 F riding)
1	Pair of shoe covers for the cold
1	Micro-bag with small night reflective vest and extra pair of ankle bands

Red crate #2 (special supplies and tools), exchanged during crew exchange

1	Complete bike tool set (cassette tool, wrenches, hex keys, chain tool, ...)
2	Bike tires
5	Bike tubes
1	Extra iodine solution bottle (in case iodine pads in hygiene backpack run out)
1	Extra jar petroleum jelly (to replace small jar in hygiene backpack if needed)
1	Extra flashlight
10	Assorted plastic bags and Ziploc bags
1	Extra front bike light, its Li battery case, and extra rear bike light in a plastic bag
1	Assorted Velcro pieces
8	Size AAA batteries (rear red light)
24	Size AA batteries (front white light)
1	Packing tape and electrical tape
1	Spare 12 V to USB/110 V car adapter, and spare amber flashlight

In each vehicle:

1	Medikit (kept in rear cup holder; Neosporin, band-aids, medical tape, ersatz skin, scissors, saddle sore pad that can be cut to size, extra numbing spray, plastic gloves)
2	Crew reflective vests
4	Crew reflective ankle bands
1	Cooler pre-stocked with 12 portions of sealed beef jerky
1	Bicycle pump
2	Amber flashing lights
1	Magnetic slow vehicle sign, including tow adapter (if vehicle is non-magnetic)
1	12 V power extender/USB with an iPhone Anker battery charge cable
2	Spare wheels with spare skewers
1	Sleeping mat (only Crew #3 vehicle)
1	Swiss army knife or equivalent multi-tool with scissors and bottle opener

Racer hygiene and rest backpack. The entire race strategy is built around daytime rest at a motel (or in an RV), and two nighttime stationary crew exchanges. Before/after rest, and while the crew is exchanging, the most important operation performed by the racer is hygiene (Chapter 7). In addition, the racer was put to bed at a motel every day except the last. All of the racer's tasks related to crew exchange and rest breaks were done with the inventory of a single backpack that the previous crew moved to the next crew vehicle, Crew #3 moved to the racer's hotel room, and Crew #1 picked up from the motel in the afternoon. The inventory of this backpack contained all small items for daily use, racer hygiene, prepping for rest, and getting up in the afternoon to race another 18 to 22 hours. The complete inventory of the backpack is listed in the table above. Note that while some of the clothes items (such as glasses, balaclava) could have been put in a milk crate, they are less likely to be lost in the backpack.

Racer hygiene backpack

Group 1: Items in daily use
1	Bag with yellow glasses, 2x brown glasses, 2x visors for night helmet
1	Heart rate monitor (always worn)
2	Emergency-item plastic bags with toilet paper, spare earbud and 300 mg caffeine tablets (middle back pocket of jersey)
1	Balaclava (night or cold weather riding)
1	Pair of white arm protectors (always worn to prevent chafing from aero pads)

Group 2: Hygiene items, used during crew exchange and during rest period
1	Sun screen spray SPF 70 (used at wakeup and during daily hygiene, as needed)
1	Towel (used to wipe off sweat, or sit on during kit changes if needed)
44	Iodine pads (4x daily hygiene: wakeup, two crew exchanges, and pre-rest)
1	Bottle mouth wash (4x daily hygiene)
1	Lip balm (4x daily hygiene)
1	Eye drops (4x daily hygiene)
3	"Wax It" benzocaine cream for topical pain relief (3x daily hygiene: wakeup and crew exchanges only)
1	Jar Vaseline (3x daily hygiene: wakeup and crew exchanges only)
1	Bottle naproxen/ibuprofen for general pain relief (3x daily hygiene: wakeup and crew exchanges only)

Group 3: Items used during or after rest period only
1	Bath kit (1 mini folding tool, comb, 3 shavers, tooth brush and paste)
1	Bottle prescription antibiotic (the racer had suffered a deep elbow wound before the race, and was finishing up a prescription from his primary care physician)
1	Bottle of Wal-som (doxylamine succinate), to help sleep if needed
11	Underwear (for rest period)
2	Short-sleeve T-shirt (for rest period)
2	Pair of socks (for rest period)
10	Nose strips (for rest period and against chafing by glasses)
2	Pair ear plugs (for rest period)
44	Large cloth adhesive bandages (wakeup only)

Group 4: Spare items at bottom of bag
1	Spare bib short, jersey, socks, and thermal upper
1	Medical tape
1	6 AA batteries, 4 AAA batteries and 2 heart rate monitor batteries

1	Extra earbud
1	Spare heart rate monitor
1	Spare charger for smartphone 6200 mAh Anker battery pack + spare battery

The first 5 items in the inventory shown above were things the racer regularly swapped, put on, or into jersey pockets during the race. They were at the top of the large back compartment of the backpack. The next 9 items were used for hygiene at wakeup, during two crew exchanges, and before rest. They were in an easily accessible small front compartment or side meshes of the backpack. The next 8 items were used to prep for the rest period or after wakeup only, and were in the medium middle compartment. The remaining items were spares in a Ziploc bag at the bottom of the large back compartment. The extra earbud and battery were both used during the race: the racer accidentally destroyed an earbud when he forgot to put it on and it got entangled in the wheels; and the crew early in the race once forgot to plug a smartphone battery into a high capacity charger, as lightweight phone chargers will not charge it.

Photo 7.6. Racer jersey layout: gel and protein/salt source on the right. Emergency-item plastic bag and official RAAM GPS in the middle. The left is reserved for smartphone GPS and battery on hot days. When used in this way, the earbud was plugged into the phone through a hole on the inside of the jersey pocket, and its cable routed inside the jersey to the ear. The emergency Ziploc bag contained paper tissue for Nature breaks, caffeine tablets, throat lozenges (useful in the dry desert air) and a spare earbud.

Preparation of jersey and other frequently used clothes. The same layout was used for the jersey each day. It is not so important what layout you pick, but it is important to pick a layout and stick to it. It reduces racer and crew errors when getting the kit ready before wakeup in the afternoon, or during crew exchanges. Photo 7.6 shows how the jersey was always stocked for us. Make sure your jersey design uses mostly light colors, or it will heat in the sun.

Two other pieces of clothing were modified for the race. First, It was clear from practices that the original thermal long-sleeved under-layer would take too long to remove, especially when it was sweaty. Thus, a long-sleeved under-layer, suitable for temperatures between 45 and 65 °F under the jersey, was slit open in the center of the back from the waist to within a few inches of the elastic neck. We called it the 'straitjacket.' The straitjacket could be put on and removed extremely rapidly by having a crew member remove and hold the jersey, have the racer slip into the straitjacket and hold the flaps in the back together, and having the crew member put the jersey back on. Finally, the racer's shoes had some holes punched into the webbing at the front top to allow better cooling and more direct evaporation from the socks. Water resistance was not an issue because the webbing was not truly waterproof anyway.

Crew supplies. The financial details are discussed in Chapter 13, but we mention here that each crew of two had a designated CFO (Chief Financial Officer), who received a pre-race check of $1500 for hotels, gas, food, and supplies before the race, and was reimbursed for additional costs afterwards. The actual cost was close to $2350 per crew, and so we now recommend pre-reimbursing the CFO $2000. The crews did have to buy all kinds of unexpected items, such as eye drops (for red-eye), and a sleeping pad (for the last rest period in the van instead of at a motel). The CFO provided the racer with full receipts for the crew after the race, and a spreadsheet listing all expenses.

The contents of the crates were tested and refined during the practice race in March 2016 (Chapter 5), as was the financial reporting scheme, the contents of the racer's hygiene bag, and the bikes and their cockpits. After refinement, the scheme described above was implemented, and worked almost flawlessly during the race. The biggest hiccup was when a crewmember stowed the spare battery in the wrong rate crate (special clothes instead of tools), and it was not found again until after the race. The crew purchased an extra battery at a Walgreens to make up for the "lost" item. The main lesson from that is to make sure that Crew #1 (before waking the racer) and/or Crew #3 (after putting the racer to bed) takes an inventory of the red crates so everything is in order.

8. RACER STRATEGY AND RACE FLOW

In this chapter, we discuss how the game plan of Chapter 2 was implemented during the 2016 race, from the perspective of the racer. The goal was to sleep the optimal number of hours—about 4 hours for a Masters racer—during the hot middle of the day, and have three 6.5 hour crew shifts move the racer forward by about 300 miles a day from late afternoon to late morning, with uninterrupted riding except for two stationary crew exchanges. This would enable the Masters racer to average the same speed as the pros (7 to 8 riding days), but with the needed extra sleep (roughly 2 rest days instead of 1).

Taper before the race It cannot be over-emphasized how important the taper period about 10-15 days before the race is. Even seasoned racers make the mistake of still cycling a lot during that time because they feel (incorrectly) that their fitness will vanish if they don't. Years of trained fitness, especially in cycling (less so in running) do not vanish during a rest period. Fitness actually increases with good sleep and as microscopic muscle damage and other stresses of training are repaired. Some key elements of the taper are as follows.

Starting about 10-15 days before the race, go to bed an hour later every day, and sleep in. For most of us this is not too hard, and it will eventually get you to where you fall asleep at 5 AM CA time and wake up at noon CA time. That is the perfect timing for mid-day sleep breaks. You'll ride through the night fresh, and you start feeling really tired in the late morning, when it's time for the roughly 4 hour mid-day rest period. Note that things can work out a little differently if you come from Europe: You are ca. 8 hours ahead of Oceanside, effectively going to bed at 3 PM CA time. Thus you need to move ahead 14 hours, which is still easier for most people than moving back 10 hours (which entails going to bed earlier every day). The Honey Badger adjusted his work schedule in summer 2016 so he could go to bed late and sleep in as the race approached. In CA, he slept from 4 AM to 11 AM the day before the start.

It is also important to stop riding hard about 10-15 days before the race. In May, the Honey Badger's volume was still over 2000 miles, but at the start of June, it dropped to *ca.* 100 miles/week. This effort was just enough to keep the legs stimulated, but allowed complete recovery compared to 300-500 mile/week volumes in the preceding months. In the 5 days before the race, while driving to California and sight-seeing, getting set up at the crew house, and registering for the race (thanks you, Deirdre Malone Greenholz!), the

Honey Badger rode only about 30 miles: the stretch from the start to where crewing starts at Old Castle Road, and a bit more towards Lake Henshaw. The latter part was done exactly as it was planned on race day, with crew #1 waiting at Old Castle Road, making a planned bike exchange, and then leapfrogging the racer for a while in the direction of Lake Henshaw. This gave the racer a small stretch of the legs and the confidence that he knew how to navigate the start of the race. It gave crew #1 a lot of confidence for the start of the race, so there would be no big surprises.

We cannot overemphasize how important it is to get good sleep, shift your sleep schedule slowly, and stop riding a lot before RAAM. One of the major problems for inexperienced RAAM racers is that they arrive at the starting line tired from last-minute riding, lack of sleep due to over-excitement, and slightly raw butt skin, ready to develop into saddle sores. When you're running a marathon, you don't do a half-marathon the day before your race. And running a marathon is a walk in the park compared to RAAM. (The author regularly runs 100+ mile running races and ran about 10 Ironmans in 2014 and 60 training marathons in 2017, so the comparison is based on experience.)

Variations from race to race For a high wattage Masters racer (1-hour functional threshold power FTP = 300 W) racing under good weather conditions (moderate desert temperatures, west wind, no storms), this means a 10-day race. For a lower wattage racer (FTP = 250 W), or a high wattage racer under less than ideal weather conditions (high desert temperatures, headwind, storms, or a combination thereof), this means an 11-day race. For a lower wattage racer under less than ideal weather conditions, this means a 12-day race and is pushing the limit of the not very generous time allowance at RAAM (see Chapter 1). Weather conditions are not under the racer's control, so one just has to barrel on as much as possible.

During the two-man team RAAM in 2013, weather conditions were essentially perfect. During solo RAAM in 2016, the temperature also cooperated, but the wind blew from the southeast for much of the Plains, and there were two major storms, including tornadoes, on the route. The result:

	2013	2016
Open male solo	7d 22h	9d 17h
Open female solo	12d 18h	11d 14h
Masters male solo	10d 22h	11d 0h
Masters female solo	11d 17h	12d 13h
Solo DNFs:	13/39 = 33%	22/42 = 52%
Open male two-man team	6d 22h	8d 10h

Even taking into account variations in racer strength and racer strategy in different years, the difference is striking: faster results in 4 out of 5 categories listed above in 2013, and only one third of racers DNF in 2013 *vs.* one half DNF in 2016. The 30% correlation of race conditions with race time discussed in Chapter 3 is by no means negligible. For this reason alone, it's a good idea to have an 11-day game plan that can be achieved even at 250 W FTP, so that one at least can finish the race in a tough year. Our racing plan adds hours to your headroom compared to the more conventional approach.

Race progression Figure 8.1 shows the progression through time stations for a 10-day race. The small vertical leaps at the red dots are the 4-hour rest breaks, where the time (hours) advances, but the distance (Miles) does not. This is one of the mentally difficult aspects of our race strategy: Racers who take shorter rest breaks will invariably be ahead of you in the early stages of the race, when they are not yet incapacitated by fatigue.

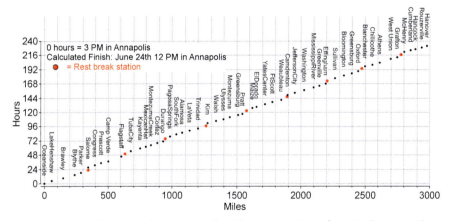

Figure 8.1. Time in hours *vs.* distance in miles. The progression is for a 10 day race. The red dots show the re-start time after a 4-hour sleep break optimized to allow mid-day sleep.

In 2016, #564 (The Honey Badger) was consistently behind #480 until time station 23 (Ulysses, KS). Even after that, #564 regularly fell behind #480 during sleep breaks as late as TS 32 (Camdenton). After that, the Honey Badger's mileage *vs.* time slope (see Figure 3.7) remained constant, while other racers' dropped off due to fatigue, and #564 increased his gap on the field up to 9 hours. Racer #492 picked a somewhat more conservative (longer) sleep strategy than #480, but not as conservative as #564. In particular, his sleep breaks were at night (riding during the hot day hours) and probably slightly too short (<3 hours) to sustain maximum pace.

Table 8.1. RAAM Time Table, 10-Day Schedule (2016 course)

TimeSt	City1	State	Miles	Hours	Speed_mph	MileTotal	Month	Day	Hour	Minute	TotalHours	rest	Crew1	Crew2	Crew3
TS00	Oceanside	CA	0	0	0	0	6	14	15	0	0	0	drive	drive	follow
TS01	LakeHenshaw	CA	56.9	4.608	12.3	56.9	6	14	19	36	4.608	0	follow	sleep	drive
TS02	Brawley	CA	88.5	4.441	19.9	145.4	6	15	0	2	9.049	0	sleep	follow	sleep
TS03	Blythe	CA	89.6	5.786	15.5	235	6	15	5	50	14.83	0	sleep	follow	follow
TS04	Parker	AZ	51.3	3.239	15.8	286.3	6	15	9	4	18.07	0	drive	drive	follow
Rest	Rest	AZ	0	5	0	340	6	15	13	4	23.07	1	follow	drive	drive
TS05	Salome	AZ	56	4.056	13.8	342.3	6	15	18	7	27.13	0	follow	sleep	drive
TS06	Congress	AZ	52.6	3.648	14.4	394.9	6	15	21	46	30.78	0	follow	sleep	sleep
TS07	Prescott	AZ	50.5	3.672	13.8	445.4	6	16	1	26	34.45	0	sleep	follow	sleep
TS08	Camp Verde	AZ	54.5	2.879	18.9	499.9	6	16	4	19	37.33	0	sleep	follow	follow
TS09	Flagstaff	AZ	102.9	7.941	13	602.8	6	16	12	16	45.27	0	drive	sleep	follow
Rest	Rest	AZ	0	5	0	630	6	16	13	45	50.27	1	follow	sleep	drive
TS10	TubaCity	AZ	75	3.98	18.8	677.8	6	16	21	15	54.25	0	follow	drive	drive
TS11	Kayenta	AZ	71.8	4.855	14.8	749.6	6	17	2	6	59.11	0	sleep	follow	sleep
TS12	MexicanHat	UT	44.6	2.451	18.2	794.2	6	17	4	33	61.56	0	sleep	follow	sleep
TS13	MontezumaCreek	UT	39.6	2.545	15.6	833.8	6	17	7	6	64.1	0	sleep	follow	sleep
TS14	Cortez	CO	50.1	3.645	13.7	883.9	6	17	10	44	67.75	0	drive	follow	follow
TS15	Durango	CO	43.9	2.825	15.5	927.8	6	17	13	34	70.57	0	drive	drive	follow
Rest	Rest	CO	0	5	0	945	6	17	15	0	75.57	1	follow	sleep	drive
TS16	PagosaSprings	CO	54.3	3.716	14.6	982.1	6	17	22	17	79.29	0	follow	drive	drive
TS17	SouthFork	CO	47.8	3.169	15.1	1029.9	6	18	1	27	82.46	0	sleep	follow	sleep
TS18	Alamosa	CO	46.6	2.763	16.9	1076.5	6	18	4	13	85.22	0	sleep	follow	sleep
TS19	LaVeta	CO	58.2	3.641	16	1134.7	6	18	7	51	88.86	0	drive	follow	follow
TS20	Trinidad	CO	65.1	3.576	18.2	1199.8	6	18	11	26	92.44	0	drive	follow	follow
Rest	Rest	CO	0	5	0	1260	6	18	15	26	97.44	1	follow	sleep	drive
TS21	Kim	CO	71.2	4.35	16.4	1271	6	18	20	47	101.8	0	follow	drive	drive
TS22	Walsh	CO	68.4	3.71	18.4	1339.4	6	19	0	29	105.5	0	sleep	follow	sleep
TS23	Ulysses	KS	53.8	3.12	17.2	1393.2	6	19	3	37	108.6	0	sleep	follow	sleep
TS24	Montezuma	KS	50.4	3.087	16.3	1443.6	6	19	6	42	111.7	0	sleep	follow	sleep
TS25	Greensburg	KS	66.1	3.933	16.8	1509.7	6	19	10	38	115.6	0	drive	drive	follow
TS26	Pratt	KS	32	1.934	16.5	1541.7	6	19	12	34	117.6	0	drive	sleep	follow
Rest	Rest	KS	0	5	0	1575	6	19	14	45	122.6	1	follow	sleep	drive
TS27	Maize	KS	76.8	4.59	16.7	1618.5	6	19	22	9	127.2	0	follow	sleep	drive
TS28	ElDorado	KS	34.2	2.139	16	1652.7	6	20	0	18	129.3	0	sleep	follow	sleep
TS29	YatesCenter	KS	64.5	3.952	16.3	1717.2	6	20	4	15	133.3	0	sleep	follow	sleep
TS30	FtScott	KS	59	3.587	16.4	1776.2	6	20	7	50	136.8	0	drive	follow	follow
TS31	Weaubleau	MO	66.3	4.209	15.8	1842.5	6	20	12	3	141.1	0	drive	drive	follow
Rest	Rest	MO	0	5	0	1890	6	20	15	3	146.1	1	follow	sleep	drive
TS32	Camdenton	MO	49	3.067	16	1891.5	6	20	20	7	149.1	0	follow	sleep	drive
TS33	JeffersonCity	MO	57.1	3.456	16.5	1948.6	6	20	23	34	152.6	0	sleep	follow	sleep
TS34	Washington	MO	76.8	4.78	16.1	2025.4	6	21	4	21	157.4	0	sleep	follow	sleep
TS35	MississippiRiver	MO	72.6	4.462	16.3	2098	6	21	8	48	161.8	0	sleep	follow	sleep
TS36	Greenville	IL	46	2.897	15.9	2144	6	21	11	42	164.7	0	drive	drive	follow
TS37	Effingham	IL	49.3	3.093	15.9	2193.3	6	21	14	48	167.8	0	drive	drive	follow
TS37	Rest	IL	0	5	0	2205	6	21	15	15	172.8	1	follow	sleep	drive
TS38	Sullivan	IN	72.7	4.474	16.2	2266	6	22	0	16	177.3	0	follow	sleep	drive
TS39	Bloomington	IN	67.3	4.341	15.5	2333.3	6	22	4	37	181.6	0	sleep	follow	sleep
TS40	Greensburg	IN	63.2	3.985	15.9	2396.5	6	22	8	36	185.6	0	sleep	follow	follow
TS41	Oxford	OH	49.6	3.083	16.1	2446.1	6	22	11	41	188.7	0	drive	drive	follow
Rest	Rest	OH	0	5	0	2475	6	22	13	30	193.7	1	follow	sleep	drive
TS42	Blanchester	OH	50.2	3.156	15.9	2496.3	6	22	19	50	196.8	0	follow	sleep	drive
TS43	Chillicothe	OH	58.1	3.519	16.5	2554.4	6	22	23	21	200.4	0	follow	sleep	sleep
TS44	Athens	OH	59.1	3.689	16	2613.5	6	23	3	3	204.1	0	sleep	follow	sleep
TS45	West Union	WY	85.6	5.525	15.5	2699.1	6	23	8	34	209.6	0	sleep	follow	follow
TS46	Grafton	WY	46.4	2.965	15.7	2745.5	6	23	11	32	212.5	0	drive	drive	follow
TS46	Rest	WY	0	5	0	2775	6	23	13	30	217.5	1	follow	sleep	drive
TS47	McHenry	WY	55.9	3.832	14.6	2801.4	6	23	20	22	221.4	0	follow	sleep	drive
TS48	Cumberland	MD	49	2.761	17.7	2850.4	6	23	23	8	224.1	0	follow	follow	sleep
TS49	Hancock	MD	37	2.196	16.9	2887.4	6	24	1	19	226.3	0	sleep	follow	sleep
TS50	Rouzerville	PA	48.5	3.1	15.6	2935.9	6	24	4	25	229.4	0	sleep	follow	sleep
TS51	Hanover	PA	40.3	2.513	16	2976.2	6	24	6	56	231.9	0	sleep	drive	follow
TS52	MtAiry	MD	36.6	2.307	15.9	3012.8	6	24	9	15	234.3	0	drive	sleep	follow
TS53	Odenton	MD	39.4	2.34	16.8	3052.2	6	24	11	35	236.6	0	drive	sleep	follow
TS54	Annapolis.	MD	9.5	0.5931	16	3061.7	6	24	12	11	237.2	0	follow	wait	follow
TS55	Finish	MD	5.8	0.4059	14.3	3067.5	6	24	12	35	237.6	0	follow	wait	follow

Table 8.2. RAAM Time Table, 11-Day Schedule (2016 course)

TimeSt	City1	State	Miles	Hours	Speed_mph	MileTotal	Month	Day	Hour	Minute	TotalHours	rest	Crew1	Crew2	Crew3
TS00	Oceanside	CA	0	0	0	0	6	14	15	0	0	0	drive	wait	follow
TS01	LakeHenshaw	CA	56.9	5.168	11	56.9	6	14	20	10	5.168	0	follow	drive	rest
TS02	Brawley	CA	88.5	4.982	17.8	145.4	6	15	1	9	10.15	0	rest	follow	rest
TS03	Blythe	CA	89.6	6.49	13.8	235	6	15	7	38	16.64	0	rest	drive	follow
TS04	Parker	AZ	51.3	3.634	14.1	286.3	6	15	11	16	20.27	0	drive	rest	follow
Rest	Rest	AZ	0	5	0	340	6	15	16	16	25.27	1	follow	rest	drive
TS05	Salome	AZ	56	4.55	12.3	342.3	6	15	20	49	29.82	0	follow	drive	drive
TS06	Congress	AZ	52.6	4.091	12.9	394.9	6	16	0	54	33.91	0	rest	follow	rest
TS07	Prescott	AZ	50.5	4.118	12.3	445.4	6	16	5	1	38.03	0	rest	follow	rest
TS08	Camp Yerde	AZ	54.5	3.23	16.9	499.9	6	16	8	15	41.26	0	drive	rest	follow
Rest	Rest	AZ	0	5	0	630	6	16	13	15	46.26	1	follow	rest	drive
TS 09	Flagstaff	AZ	102.9	8.907	11.6	602.8	6	16	22	10	55.17	0	follow	drive	rest
TS 10	TubaCity	AZ	75	4.465	16.8	677.8	6	17	2	38	59.63	0	rest	follow	rest
TS11	Kayenta	AZ	71.8	5.446	13.2	749.6	6	17	8	4	65.08	0	rest	drive	follow
TS12	MexicanHat	UT	44.6	2.75	16.2	794.2	6	17	10	49	67.83	0	drive	rest	rest
TS13	MontezumaCreek	UT	39.6	2.855	13.9	833.8	6	17	13	41	70.69	0	drive	rest	follow
Rest	Rest	CO	0	5	0	945	6	17	18	41	75.69	1	follow	rest	drive
TS14	Cortez	CO	50.1	4.089	12.3	883.9	6	17	22	46	79.77	0	follow	drive	drive
TS15	Durango	CO	43.9	3.169	13.9	927.8	6	18	1	56	82.94	0	rest	follow	rest
TS16	PagosaSprings	CO	54.3	4.168	13	982.1	6	18	6	6	87.11	0	rest	follow	rest
TS17	SouthFork	CO	47.8	3.555	13.4	1029.9	6	18	9	39	90.67	0	drive	rest	follow
TS18	Alamosa	CO	46.6	3.099	15	1076.5	6	18	12	45	93.76	0	drive	rest	follow
Rest	Rest	CO	0	5	0	1260	6	18	17	45	98.76	1	follow	rest	drive
TS19	LaYeta	CO	58.2	4.084	14.3	1134.7	6	18	21	50	102.8	0	follow	drive	drive
TS20	Trinidad	CO	65.1	4.011	16.2	1199.8	6	19	1	51	106.9	0	rest	follow	rest
TS21	Kim	CO	71.2	4.88	14.6	1271	6	19	6	44	111.7	0	rest	drive	rest
TS22	Walsh	CO	68.4	4.161	16.4	1339.4	6	19	10	54	115.9	0	drive	drive	follow
TS23	Ulysses	KS	53.8	3.499	15.4	1393.2	6	19	14	23	119.4	0	drive	rest	follow
Rest	Rest	KS	0	5	0	1575	6	19	19	23	124.4	1	follow	rest	drive
TS24	Montezuma	KS	50.4	3.463	14.6	1443.6	6	19	22	51	127.9	0	follow	drive	rest
TS25	Greensburg	KS	66.1	4.411	15	1509.7	6	20	3	16	132.3	0	rest	follow	rest
TS26	Pratt	KS	32	2.17	14.7	1541.7	6	20	5	26	134.4	0	rest	drive	follow
TS27	Maize	KS	76.8	5.148	14.9	1618.5	6	20	10	35	139.6	0	drive	rest	follow
Rest	Rest	MO	0	5	0	1890	6	20	15	35	144.6	1	follow	rest	drive
TS29	YatesCenter	KS	64.5	4.433	14.5	1717.2	6	20	20	1	149	0	follow	drive	drive
TS30	FtScott	KS	59	4.024	14.7	1776.2	6	21	0	2	153	0	rest	follow	rest
TS31	Weaubleau	MO	66.3	4.721	14	1842.5	6	21	4	46	157.8	0	rest	follow	rest
TS32	Camdenton	MO	49	3.44	14.2	1891.5	6	21	8	12	161.2	0	drive	drive	follow
TS33	JeffersonCity	MO	57.1	3.877	14.7	1948.6	6	21	12	5	165.1	0	drive	rest	follow
Rest	Rest	MO	0	5	0	1890	6	21	17	5	170.1	1	follow	rest	drive
TS34	Washington	MO	76.8	5.362	14.3	2025.4	6	21	22	27	175.5	0	follow	drive	rest
TS35	MississippiRiver	MO	72.6	5.004	14.5	2098	6	22	3	27	180.5	0	rest	follow	rest
TS36	Greenville	IL	46	3.249	14.2	2144	6	22	6	42	183.7	0	rest	drive	follow
TS37	Effingham	IL	49.3	3.469	14.2	2193.3	6	22	10	10	187.2	0	drive	rest	follow
Rest	Rest	IL	0	5	0	2205	6	22	15	10	192.2	1	follow	rest	drive
TS38	Sullivan	IN	72.7	5.019	14.5	2266	6	22	20	11	197.2	0	follow	drive	drive
TS39	Bloomington	IN	67.3	4.869	13.8	2333.3	6	23	1	3	202.1	0	rest	follow	rest
TS40	Greensburg	IN	63.2	4.47	14.1	2396.5	6	23	5	31	206.5	0	rest	follow	rest
TS41	Oxford	OH	49.6	3.459	14.3	2446.1	6	23	8	59	210	0	drive	drive	follow
TS42	Blanchester	OH	50.2	3.54	14.2	2496.3	6	23	12	31	213.5	0	drive	rest	follow
Rest	Rest	OH	0	5	0	2475	6	23	17	31	218.5	1	follow	rest	drive
TS43	Chillicothe	OH	58.1	3.947	14.7	2554.4	6	23	21	28	222.5	0	follow	drive	rest
TS44	Athens	OH	59.1	4.138	14.3	2613.5	6	24	1	36	226.6	0	rest	follow	rest
TS45	West Union	WV	85.6	6.198	13.8	2699.1	6	24	7	48	232.8	0	rest	follow	rest
TS46	Grafton	WV	46.4	3.325	14	2745.5	6	24	11	8	236.1	0	drive	rest	follow
TS46	Rest	WV	0	5	0	2775	6	24	16	8	241.1	1	follow	rest	drive
TS47	McHenry	WV	55.9	4.299	13	2801.4	6	24	20	26	245.4	0	follow	drive	drive
TS48	Cumberland	MD	49	3.097	15.8	2850.4	6	24	23	31	248.5	0	follow	drive	rest
TS49	Hancock	MD	37	2.463	15	2887.4	6	25	1	59	251	0	rest	follow	rest
TS50	Rouzerville	PA	48.5	3.477	13.9	2935.9	6	25	5	28	254.5	0	rest	follow	rest
TS51	Hanover	PA	40.3	2.819	14.3	2976.2	6	25	8	17	257.3	0	drive	follow	follow
TS52	MtAiry	MD	36.6	2.588	14.1	3012.8	6	25	10	52	259.9	0	drive	rest	follow
TS53	Odenton	MD	39.4	2.625	15	3052.2	6	25	13	30	262.5	0	wait	rest	follow
TS54	Annapolis.	MD	9.5	0.6653	14.3	3061.7	6	25	14	10	263.2	0	wait	rest	follow
TS55	Finish	MD	5.8	0.4553	12.7	3067.5	6	25	14	37	263.6	0	wait	wait	follow

Table 8.3. RAAM Time Table, 12+ Day Schedule (2018 course)

TimeSt	City1	State	Miles	Hours	Speed_mph	MileTotal	Month	Day	Hour	Minute	TotalHours	rest
TS00	Oceanside	CA	0	0		0	6	14	15	0	0	0
TS01	LakeHenshaw	CA	56.9	5.742	9.91	56.9	6	14	20	44	5.742	0
TS02	Brawley	CA	88.5	5.534	16	145.4	6	15	2	16	11.28	0
TS03	Blythe	CA	89.6	7.21	12.4	235	6	15	9	29	18.49	0
TS04	Parker	AZ	51.3	4.037	12.7	286.3	6	15	13	31	22.52	0
Rest	Rest	AZ	0	5.5	0	286.3	6	15	19	1	28.02	1
TS05	Salome	AZ	56	5.055	11.1	342.3	6	16	0	4	33.08	0
TS06	Congress	AZ	52.6	4.546	11.6	394.9	6	16	4	37	37.62	0
TS07	Prescott	AZ	50.5	4.575	11	445.4	6	16	9	11	42.2	0
TS08	Camp Verde	AZ	54.5	3.588	15.2	499.9	6	16	12	47	45.79	0
Rest	Rest	AZ	0	5.5	0	499.9	6	16	18	17	51.29	1
TS 09	Flagstaff	AZ	102.9	9.896	10.4	602.8	6	17	4	11	61.18	0
TS 10	TubaCity	AZ	75	4.96	15.1	677.8	6	17	9	8	66.14	0
Rest	Rest	AZ	0	5	0	677.8	6	17	14	8	71.14	1
TS11	Kayenta	AZ	71.8	6.051	11.9	749.6	6	17	20	11	77.19	0
TS12	MexicanHat	UT	44.6	3.055	14.6	794.2	6	17	23	14	80.25	0
TS13	MontezumaCreek	UT	39.6	3.172	12.5	833.8	6	18	2	25	83.42	0
TS14	Cortez	CO	50.1	4.543	11	883.9	6	18	6	57	87.96	0
TS15	Durango	CO	43.9	3.52	12.5	927.8	6	18	10	29	91.48	0
TS16	PagosaSprings	CO	54.3	4.631	11.7	982.1	6	18	15	6	96.12	0
Rest	Rest	CO	0	5.5	0	982.1	6	18	20	36	101.6	1
TS17	SouthFork	CO	47.8	3.949	12.1	1029.9	6	19	0	33	105.6	0
TS18	Alamosa	CO	46.6	3.443	13.5	1076.5	6	19	4	0	109	0
TS19	LaVeta	CO	58.2	4.538	12.8	1134.7	6	19	8	32	113.5	0
Rest	Rest	CO	0	5	0	1134.7	6	19	13	32	118.5	1
TS20	Trinidad	CO	65.1	4.456	14.6	1199.8	6	19	18	0	123	0
TS21	Kim	CO	71.2	5.421	13.1	1271	6	19	23	25	128.4	0
TS22	Walsh	CO	68.4	4.623	14.8	1339.4	6	20	4	2	133	0
TS23	Ulysses	KS	53.8	3.888	13.8	1393.2	6	20	7	55	136.9	0
TS24	Montezuma	KS	50.4	3.847	13.1	1443.6	6	20	11	46	140.8	0
Rest	Rest	KS	0	5	0	1443.6	6	20	16	46	145.8	1
TS25	Greensburg	KS	66.1	4.901	13.5	1509.7	6	20	21	40	150.7	0
TS26	Pratt	KS	32	2.41	13.3	1541.7	6	21	0	5	153.1	0
TS27	Maize	KS	76.8	5.72	13.4	1618.5	6	21	5	48	158.8	0
TS29	YatesCenter	KS	64.5	4.925	13.1	1683	6	21	10	44	163.7	0
Rest	Rest	KS	0	4.5	0	1683	6	21	15	14	168.2	1
TS30	FtScott	KS	59	4.47	13.2	1742	6	21	19	42	172.7	0
TS31	Weaubleau	MO	66.3	5.245	12.6	1808.3	6	22	0	57	178	0
TS32	Camdenton	MO	49	3.822	12.8	1857.3	6	22	4	46	181.8	0
TS33	JeffersonCity	MO	57.1	4.307	13.3	1914.4	6	22	9	4	186.1	0
Rest	Rest	MO	0	4.5	0	1914.4	6	22	13	34	190.6	1
TS34	Washington	MO	76.8	5.957	12.9	1991.2	6	22	19	32	196.5	0
TS35	MississippiRiver	MO	72.6	5.56	13.1	2063.8	6	23	1	5	202.1	0
TS36	Greenville	IL	46	3.61	12.7	2109.8	6	23	4	42	205.7	0
TS37	Effingham	IL	49.3	3.854	12.8	2159.1	6	23	8	33	209.6	0
Rest	Rest	IL	0	5	0	2159.1	6	23	13	33	214.6	1
TS38	Sullivan	IN	72.7	5.576	13	2231.8	6	23	19	8	220.1	0
TS39	Bloomington	IN	67.3	5.409	12.4	2299.1	6	24	0	32	225.5	0
TS40	Greensburg	IN	63.2	4.966	12.7	2362.3	6	24	5	30	230.5	0
TS41	Oxford	OH	49.6	3.842	12.9	2411.9	6	24	9	21	234.4	0
TS42	Blanchester	OH	50.2	3.933	12.8	2462.1	6	24	13	17	238.3	0
TS42	Rest	OH	0	5	0	2462.1	6	24	18	17	243.3	1
TS43	Chillicothe	OH	58.1	4.385	13.3	2520.2	6	24	22	40	247.7	0
TS44	Athens	OH	59.1	4.597	12.9	2579.3	6	25	3	16	252.3	0
TS45	West Union	WV	85.6	6.886	12.4	2664.9	6	25	10	9	259.2	0
TS46	Grafton	WV	46.4	3.695	12.6	2711.3	6	25	13	51	262.9	0
TS46	Rest	WV	0	4.5	0	2711.3	6	25	18	51	267.9	1
TS47	McHenry	WV	55.9	4.776	11.7	2767.2	6	25	23	37	272.6	0
TS48	Cumberland	MD	49	3.44	14.2	2816.2	6	26	3	4	276.1	0
TS49	Hancock	MD	37	2.736	13.5	2853.2	6	26	5	48	278.8	0
TS50	Rouzerville	PA	48.5	3.863	12.6	2901.7	6	26	9	40	282.7	0
TS51	Hanover	PA	40.3	3.132	12.9	2942	6	26	12	48	285.8	0
TS52	MtAiry	MD	36.6	2.875	12.7	2978.6	6	26	15	40	288.7	0
TS53	Odenton	MD	39.4	2.916	13.5	3018	6	26	18	35	291.6	0
TS54	Annapolis	MD	9.5	0.7392	12.9	3027.5	6	26	19	19	292.3	0
TS55	Finish	MD	5.8	0.5058	11.5	3033.3	6	26	19	50	292.8	0

The first sleep break for #492 was at 35 hours instead of #564's 22 hours, and this is especially draining before attempting the difficult high altitude, low oxygen climbs in the Rockies. As a result, #492 ended up between #564 and #480. We emphasize again here that the differences among finish times are unlikely to be due to large functional threshold output power differences. The Masters riders were all strong ultracyclists (see analysis in Chapter 3). More likely, the differences are due to fatigue and heat exposure resulting from different race strategies (Chapter 2).

Optimal scheduling. Tables 8.1, 8.2 and 8.3 embody all **5 keystones** of our race strategy:

1. The Master racer sleeps about 4 hours per day.
2. The racer jet-lags to sleep in the middle of the day, when it is hottest.
3. Race uninterrupted for 19-21 hours through the night until late morning.
4. Make use of stationary crew exchanges for two racer hygiene breaks.
5. Three crew vehicles keeps two crew in each rested with 6-7 hour shifts.

Table 8.1 shows the calculated times from between time stations for the 10-day race schedule corresponding to Figure 8.1. Table 8.2 shows the same information for an 11-day race schedule, appropriate for the strongest Master riders when the weather does not cooperate, or lower power riders under good conditions. Table 8.3 shows a 12+ day schedule, useful for some Masters Women racers or Grandmasters racers. The tables assume that the racer can ramp up the heart rate to 160-age while climbing. It will be lower during descents and flat riding, especially later in the race, when the central governor puts limits on energy expenditure, and even caffeine no longer works very well.

The tables above list the following information: Time station number; name of time station; state of time station; miles at time station; hours to get to the time station; average speed from previous time station; total mileage up to the time station; month/day/hour/minute of arrival at the time station; total hours raced; riding=0 and resting=1; Crew #1/2/3 drive/follow/sleep cycles. Note that the nominal start time listed is 15:00 Eastern Daylight Savings Time, or noon in California. Due to RAW starts and staggered solo starts, the actual start time from Oceanside is more likely after 13:00 local time. Note that Table 8.3 would result in a DNF in the Male Open or Masters categories. It does however provide extra sleep breaks in the tough desert and mountain segments early on, perfect for maintaining strength later in the race for racers that qualify for the 12+ day schedule.

The times and speeds in the Tables take into account terrain, prevailing winds, temperatures and altitude. The rest breaks are simply listed before the closest time station, and should be held at a time that sticks to the sleep schedule (about 13:00 to 17:00 at the end of the race on the East Coast, about 10:00 to 14:00 local CA time at the beginning on the west coast). Sleep breaks are not necessarily at a time station. The crew activity cycles are a very rough indication because crew shifts do not usually line up with time stations, but should be divided roughly into 6- to 7-hour intervals, or about 95- to 110-mile shifts (shorter on steep terrain). The average daily crew routine is laid out in more detail in the table in Chapter 9.

Effect of deviating from the sleep schedule The Honey Badger started out on the 10-day schedule in 2016, feasible if there were enough west wind in the plains, and if night-riding kept the temperature comfortable. When our racer emerged from the last climb in the Rockies in Trinidad after 4 days of racing, he was about 4 hours behind the 10-day schedule. It would have been possible to make up this time in flat eastern Colorado and Kansas with a west wind. Unfortunately, the winds were cross- and headwinds for the next 800 miles, and it was clear from the wind forecast even before reaching TS 20 at Trinidad that we would fall further behind and needed to switch to the 11-day schedule.

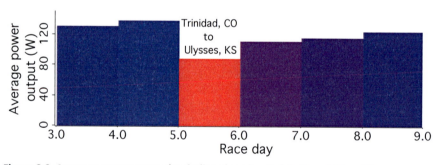

Figure 8.2. Average output power (excluding sleep breaks) in the middle of the race.

The four-hour delay into Trinidad put the Honey Badger well beyond his ability to overcome jetlag. He ended up sleeping little or not at all at the motel in Trinidad. The result the next day was a large drop in sustainable output power, as shown in Figure 8.2 (see also Chapter 3). Fortunately, our crew chief decreed a short riding day (only 200 miles to Ulysses, KS) and an extra hour of sleep for the next shift. The shorter riding day saved the situation in several ways. It put our racer back on a mid-day sleep schedule, avoiding too much riding in the heat. It also returned the crews to their normal driving and sleeping schedules. Finally, as a result of a full 5-hour sleep in Ulysses, the Honey Badger recovered his 10-day sustainable output power of *ca.* 120 W over the next few days (see also Day 5–Day 6 sleep in Figure 3.8 in Chapter 3). Other Masters racers were trying to do the whole race on minimal or irregular short sleep breaks, and probably suffered a breakdown of their output power early on, and were unable to recover from it because the pattern was repeated for too long. Clearly, our racer came close to a collapse of output power by just tempting fate once at the end of Day 4 in Trinidad.

Racer feeding schedule. Consistent food intake is very important during a 10+ day race.[16] The Honey Badger lost about 5 pounds of fat during the race, less than half a pound per day, and remained fully hydrated for most of the race except for the second day in Arizona. The fat loss was estimated several days after the race, when the racer had clearly re-hydrated. At 100-110 beats per minute (or 160-age in general), a racer burns between 6500 kcal (flat terrain) and 9000 kcal (climbing) per day. As a guide, actual calorie expenditures (based on heart rate) and average speed for each day of the 2016 race are listed in Table 8.4 for the 143 pound Honey Badger.

Table 8.4. Racer #564 daily progress, calorie expenditure, speed and climbing data for RAAM 2016.

Day	Dist.	Energy expenditure, kcal	On-bike speed, mph	Elevation gain, ft.	Segment raced
1	345 mi.	13000	18.7	16300	Oceanside to Salome
2	262 mi.	9300	14.4	21200	Salome to Flagstaff
3	328 mi.	7700	16.8	21900	Flagstaff to Durango
4	278 mi.	9000	15.4	18200	Durango to Trinidad
5	195 mi.	6500	18.0	3400	Trinidad to Ulysses
6	328 mi.	7300	17.9	6900	Ulysses to Yates Center
7	295 mi.	7300	16.8	19700	Yates Center to Rosebud
8	293 mi.	7900	16.2	8400	Rosebud to Linton
9	276 mi.	6200	15.8	13800	Linton to Chillicothe
10	238 mi.	6200	14.2	19000	Chillicothe to Oakland
11	285 mi.	8000	13.9	21200	Oakland to Annapolis
Avg.	281 mi.	8000	16.2	15455	Oceanside to Annapolis

The average caloric loss is about 8000 kcal/day. A typical racer can ingest about 300 kcal/hour on a cool day, about 250 on average, and about 200 on a hot day, and the Honey Badger falls in that range. Each crew shift, he typically took in three 100 kcal gels, two 100-kcal energy bars, five 150-kcal bottles, and one 450-kcal 6" sub sandwich. This amounts to about 260 kcal/hour on average, which right in the sustainable range. As expected, the racer took in less during very hot stretches (e.g. Arizona on Day 2), and more towards the cooler end of the race on the East Coast (days 8-11). In addition, he ate a granola breakfast of about 400 kcal after getting up each afternoon, and an 800-kcal meal (usually a pizza, chicken wrap, or similar food with a soft drink) before the rest period. The total intake was thus about 6300 kcal/day, and the deficit over the whole race about 11 x 1700 = 18700 kcal. A typical literature estimate for the weight equivalent of a pound of fat is 3500 kcal,[17] and 18700/3500 ≈ 5 pounds, a close match to the actual weight loss measured after the race. Thus, we believe that this is a near-optimal feeding schedule, as the racer would slow down due to digestive problems with higher caloric intake, and lose excessive weight with lower caloric intake.

The energy drink consumed was a 50:50 mix of HEED and Gatorade powder, which provides a tolerable mix of simple sugars and longer-chain carbohydrates for the Honey Badger. Lighter-tasting drink mixes with a better salt-carbohydrate balance include Tailwind, which reduces the need for salt caps during the race. Other racers may prefer a 100% gel and liquid diet, but Martin required solid food for the stomach to remain settled over long periods of time, and for that reason, chose energy bars and sandwiches. The bars ranged from Rice Krispies Treats to Kind nut bars. The sandwiches were low fat protein/carbohydrate combinations, such as chicken subs. The protein/carbohydrate mixture in meals was important for both palatability and for improving muscle glycogen storage.[18] Everything was eaten on the bike without stopping, except for dinner and breakfast, which were consumed during the rest stop.

One final observation can be made in Table 8.4. On Day 2, a heavy climbing day with 20200 ft., the Honey Badger averaged 14.4 mph. On Day 11, another heavy climbing day with 20200 ft., the Honey Badger averaged 13.9 mph. Thus, about 0.5 mph was lost to fatigue despite all the care taken with food and sleep. Likewise, the heart rate dropped from 110 early in the race to 80 on the last part of the last day. The late decline was most likely due to insufficient sleep after Day 10, and no afternoon sleep on Day 11, a strong reminder not to attempt low sleep early in the race, where the consequences will have a much larger effect. A speed difference of "only" 0.5 mph, over 19.5 hours a day for 10 days, amounts to nearly 100 miles lost, or about 6 to 7 extra hours in the rolling terrain 100 miles before the finish line. Insufficient calorie intake or sleep deprivation quickly add up.

Racer caffeination schedule. As discussed in the race report in Chapter 12, as well as Crew #2 operations in Chapter 9, caffeine can be of great help in very long endurance races, where extreme fatigue plays a big role and the central governor can shut down muscle fiber recruitment. However, caffeine is a double-edged sword for the Masters RAAM racer: take too little too soon, and the effect will be minimal, especially later in the race. Take too much too late, and you won't be able to sleep for 4 hours mid-day.

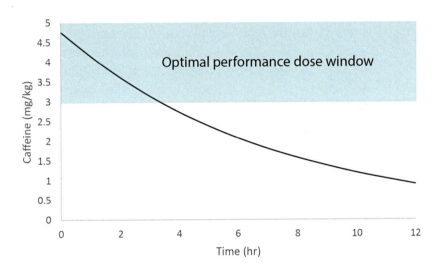

Figure 8.3. Caffeine in the racer's system for a 63 kg individual taking a 300 mg dose.

Although the literature still debates whether one becomes habituated to caffeine,[19] or whether it works even for those who consume a lot already, the Honey Badger found that the effect of caffeine certainly declines from day to day when it is used over and over again. Thus we recommend holding off on caffeine use during the race for as long as possible. With a 4-hour, 2-REM cycle sleep each day, this should be possible until more than halfway through the race, e.g. Day 6 or 7.

When dosing,[20,21]

- don't dose until the racer gets very tired and slows down, typically the early morning hours of the Crew #2 shift;

- stay in the effective window, which has a maximum based on literature (Figure 8.3). Change the dose in the proper ratio from 300 mg, depending on whether your body weight is greater or smaller than The Honey Badger's 63 kg;
- after about 5 hours, the blood serum concentration will fall, and caffeine needs to be re-dosed with about 100 mg (in the example of Figure 8.3). Do not take too much: it can cause dizziness, and the racer will not be able to sleep during his or her mid-day break.

Following these guidelines, re-dosing will often occur in the mid-morning, just a few hours before the racer is to go to sleep. One re-dosing is the maximum recommended, so the racer can do the all-important mid-day sleep. In addition, the racer could take a tablet of diphenhydramine or doxylamine about 45 minutes before the planned rest. These generic sleepiness-inducing antihistamines are not on the WADA banned list. But beware: they make you drowsy (that's the whole idea), which is dangerous on the bike. Never use anything during a race, be it as simple as ibuprofen or doxylamine or caffeine, unless you have found the proper dosing for these over-the-counter remedies.

Racer hygiene schedule. One of the most important items for the racer to take care of was hygiene, as has been stressed throughout this book. The crotch and seat bone areas are subject to saddle pressure and mild chafing even with the best chamois cream and best saddles one can find (Chapter 5). The Honey Badger implemented the same hygiene procedure four times each day: after getting up, during the two crew changes, and before going to bed. The necessary materials were in the racer's backpack, which the crews switched from vehicle to vehicle to motel, and which always stayed with the racer (see Chapter 7 for inventory):

a. Dab sensitive areas with an iodine-povidone pad, available in single-use packs
b. Apply "Wax-It" or similar long-action benzocaine cream over sensitive areas
c. Apply antibiotic cream
d. Apply vaseline-shea butter combination, or your favorite chamois cream
e. Put on fresh bib shorts if it was hot (generally after the first shift, not after the second shift)
f. Take ibuprofen to reduce inflammation
g. Rinse mouth with antibacterial mouth wash
h. Apply lip balm
i. Apply eye drops

The whole procedure takes about 10 minutes, and was carried out in or near the next crew's van during each stationary crew exchange (see Chapter 9), which also required about 10 minutes.

What is the purpose of each hygiene step? Step a. is important because it kills bacteria very efficiently, even if they are antibiotic-resistant. It was the main line of defense against saddle sores. Step b. serves solely to numb pain. Step c. is a secondary measure to reduce bacterial growth. Step d. reduces friction, and others can substitute their favorite lubricant, from bag balm to the chamois cream of your choice. Step e. is important if the racer sweated into the bib shorts to any significant extent, and also provides a different bib with different pressure points, as each crew had its own different brand bib (see Chapter 7). Step f. is necessary due to the enormous strain on knees, ankles, back, and the seating area. The Honey Badger found that recovery is much faster when inflammation is reduced, by comparing systematically with/without anti-inflammatory regimens during a 3-year training period. Inflammation is a first-line response of the innate immune system that activates destructive free radicals. The response evolved to combat tissue-invading bacteria before the T-cell immune system has a chance to act. The inflammation during racing has nothing to do with bacteria, and peroxide and other substances released by the inflammation response simply do unnecessary damage in stressed joints. Humans did not evolve to run two-hour marathons or cycle 3000 miles, and some of our defense mechanisms simply do more harm than good in such situations. Step g. is necessary to combat canker sores, which the racer tends to develop when eating a sugary diet day after day. The origin of canker sores is still under dispute, although *Helicobacter pylori*, responsible for stomach ulcers, is a possible agent, as is a viral infection. Whatever the cause may be, extensive with/without mouthwash regimens during 3 years of training proved conclusively that canker sores appear within about 2-3 days of a sugary diet under racing stress when no mouthwash is used, and never appear when antibacterial mouthwash is used. 2016 RAAM was no exception: the Honey Badger used mouthwash four times a day and never suffered from mouth sores. Steps h. and i. were necessary due to the dry desert and mountain altitudes. Indeed, Martin failed to use eye drops for the first two days, and paid for it with red-eye (conjunctivitis) that took several days of regularly using eye drops and waiting for it to clear up.

Shaving. This is a traditional rite of passage for road cyclists, although many ultracyclists don't bother. Our racer normally does not shave, but he shaved *completely* the day before the race: legs all the way up to the inseam and in the inseam; arms all the way; chest. The reason was purely for utility:

a. The hygiene procedure outlined above is facilitated by shaving all the way up the inseam. Care should be taken not to nick the skin in the inseam.

b. Application and removal of bandages is greatly eased and sped up. This includes preventative bandages (e.g. over nipples, which chafe easily in the desert heat), as well as bandaging for wounds (e.g. road rash).

c. We used a plastic bag around shoe and ankle, sealed above the ankle with duct tape, in combination with non-tearing pedals, for complete rain protection of the feet. Shaving makes tape removal much easier.

d. Application of sun screen in copious amounts, necessary especially for the desert stages, is facilitated by shaved limbs.

In addition, there may be a non-negligible aerodynamic advantage. Specialized Bicycles has performed wind tunnel tests on actual riders that translate into a 50 to 80 second time gain in a 25 mile time trial at 25 mph. Without getting into the equations, drag is linearly proportional to speed. Thus a similar savings can be expected for slower riders on a mileage basis: you save less when going slower, but you also ride longer so the savings go on for longer. Our author confirmed the Specialized numbers anecdotally on multiple 100 mile rides, ridden at similar average output power with and without shaved legs: about 5 minutes are saved per 100 miles ridden at speeds in the 17 to 22 mph range. Over a 3000 mile race, this translates into 2.5 hours gained, not a negligible effect. At the 2013 two-man team RAAM, the author might have come in second place instead of third, had he and his team mate shaved their legs.

Racer rest schedule. Each day our racer would arrive at a hotel between 10:00 and 14:00 (except at Trinidad, where we arrived 4 hours late and a 'reset' was required to move the rest schedule back to mid-day.) Crew #3 often took Martin to the same motel where Crew #2 was resting. This has the added advantage that if something is wrong with the racer's room, a room is guaranteed to be available. Martin went through the same hygiene steps as during exchanges, with some modifications.

At the start of the rest break:

a. Shower and soap sensitive areas
b. Dab with iodine-povidone pad, available in single-use packs
c. Apply antibiotic cream
d. Apply lip balm
e. Apply eye drops
f. Eat quick pre-arranged meal and hydrate

g. Brush teeth
h. Rinse mouth with antibacterial mouth wash

In addition, Martin had earplugs (and many spares) to facilitate deeper sleep. Most motels had reasonable shades that could be drawn, but a pair of sleep blinders for the eyes could also be considered. Just before going to bed, Martin hydrated and ate a quick 'dinner,' such as a wrap, a pizza, or a sandwich. Another bedtime item to consider, especially if your digestion is sensitive to dehydration: fiber capsules or a stool softener. We used them after the first 2 or 3 days to play it safe. Race food is not very high in fiber and can lead to constipation when the racer is dehydrated.

At the end of rest break:

a. Eat granola breakfast laid out by Crew #3 before waking up racer
b. Brush teeth
c. Rinse mouth with antibacterial mouth wash
d. Dab with iodine-povidone pad, available in single-use packs
e. Apply "Wax-It" or similar long-action benzocaine cream over sensitive areas
f. Apply antibiotic cream
g. Apply vaseline-shea butter combination or favorite chamois cream
h. Apply SPF 70 sunscreen to face, neck, arms and legs ALWAYS
i. Put on fresh bib shorts provided by Crew #1
j. Take 600 to 800 mg ibuprofen to reduce inflammation
k. Apply lip balm
l. Apply eye drops
m. Apply 2 band-aids: 2 to forehead, and 1 one between each thumb and index finger
n. Put on rest of kit: gloves, arm protectors, and jersey with pockets stocked.

By having the crew lay out everything in a line on the motel room desk or floor, it was easy to go through the steps each time in a few minutes and without error. The training race, and a checklist for the crew could help here. The jersey was stocked before wakeup by Crew #3 with the RAAM GPS transponder, the emergency zip-loc bag (see inventory and photo 7.6 in Chapter 7), and lip balm in middle pocket, and a gel flask and beef jerky for the whole shift in the right pocket. The left pocket was reserved for the smartphone GPS and its battery, to avoid overheating it when the temperature was too high.

As can be seen in point m., the Honey Badger applied 4 large cloth bandages at the end of each rest period: two to the forehead, and one between the thumb and index finger of each hand under the gloves. Sunscreen cannot be applied to the forehead because sweat entrains it into the eyes. Two band-aids on the forehead therefore prevented a "vent tan" from the helmet vents. Even with the best gloves, the skin between the thumb and index finger chafes when the rider is not in the aero position. A non-aero position is used frequently in a race with 170,000 feet of climbing. Strategically applied band-aids kept the Honey Badger's hands completely chafe-free for the whole race. For the same reason, the arm protectors (white compression sleeves) listed under n. were worn almost without exception all day, so there was little searching for them in the hygiene bag during the race.

The end result of all the hygiene procedures during crew exchanges and rest breaks was that the racer never suffered from any saddle sores, developed no mouth sores from the sugary diet, had no blisters on his hands, and felt relatively refreshed each day by showering and brushing teeth regularly during the race.

The value of small creature comforts is not to be underestimated. We credit them for the Martin doing relatively little fidgeting until the last day of the race: fidgeting is when racers constantly stop to adjust this and that, or request such and such, just to avoid riding. It can be seen in Figure 3.8 that our racer did more of it on Day 11 (many short dips in speed are the key signature), but this phenomenon often appears on Day 3 or 4 for other racers. Fidgeting can cost a lot of time if it starts early on. Yet even the best attention to the seating area could not completely prevent chafing and sit bone pressure pain after 10 or 11 days, resulting in some fidgeting by our racer.

Race flow. The racer had very few idle breaks besides the main sleep break and short hygiene breaks during crew exchange. Unplanned breaks were usually related to weather, flat tires, empty batteries for lights or electronics, and in one case a parade in a small town. Continuous riding for 18 to 22 hours with a good average on-bike speed was important to keep on schedule (see Table 8.3 for actual daily on-bike averages). As a result, the racer fulfilled **keystone 3** of the book's strategy: to ride as fast on average as the top three Open male racers (*ca.* 8 days, 16 hours on the bike in 2016), while sleeping longer than the Open male racers (2+ days total instead of 1+ day total). This is to be contrasted with some other Masters racers in 2016 (Figure 3.9), who spent a day more riding and a day less sleeping, by attempting sleep schedules similar to the younger Open male racers. In essence, other master racers *replaced sleeping by riding without any overall time gains*, leading to excessive fatigue at the end of the race, and perhaps a much more painful race experience.

Note that the Day 1 schedule in Table 8.4 shows a particularly long ride at the beginning, when the racer was fresh. This was planned as a result of the race start, which occurs right when the racer should be sleeping. Instead, the racer went to bed earlier and got up earlier just before the race (11:00 California time), and rode longer to get on the 10:00 to 14:00 (CA time) or 13:00 to 17:00 (Annapolis time) sleep schedule. Likewise, the racer slept less on Day 10 and not at all on Day 11, which included as much climbing as the toughest days in the Rockies. These choices are discussed in more detail in Chapter 11.

Those aspects of the race flow centered around the rest period and stationary crew exchanges are discussed in more detail in the next chapter. In this chapter, we conclude with optimal deployment of the bicycles.

Choice of bicycles. As discussed in Chapter 7, we had four bicycles to choose from during the race. One (the CTT) was not used, and brought along only as an emergency backup. The others were ridden at various times during the race, depending on terrain and wind conditions. Figure 8.4 shows an elevation map of the course together with time stations, and the choice of bike employed at each stage of the race. The main bike that was ridden is listed, and the parentheses show the alternate bike available in the active crew van. The crew planned bicycle exchanges to make the best bike choices available as much as possible, and succeeded with at least one of the two bikes 100% of the time, and with two about 80% of the time.

As a reminder, the Merlin is a very light titanium frame with low profile rims and no aerobar, intended for climbing. The superbike is an aerodynamic time trial beam bike that offers maximum comfort and speed in aero position for flat or descending terrain with small rollers, and into headwinds. The TCR0 is an all-around bike with road handlebars and clip-on aerobars, best on mixed rollers and slight climbing terrain.

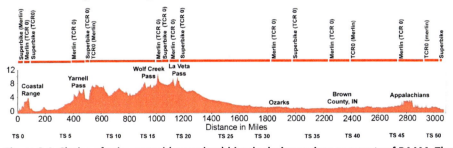

Figure 8.4. Choice of primary and (secondary) bicycle during various segments of RAAM. The bicycles are identified in the Figure 7.2 in Chapter 7. Elevation units: 1000s of feet.

It is worth noting that Figure 8.4 does not show all that many bicycle exchanges. The reason is that they are time-costly. If it takes 3 minutes to stop and swap bikes, the racer must ride at least 1 mph faster for an hour to make up the time lost. This is unlikely to happen every hour. (The Dimond Superbike buys about 1.5 mph over the Merlin on flat terrain in a 10 mph headwind and 20 mph riding speed; the difference between the TCR0 and the other two bikes is even smaller). Thus, we adopted a strategy of making sure an optimal or near-optimal bike was ridden over longer stretches, often 2 days in a row, such as the Superbike in the central plains. The longer-term strategy also made it easier for the crew to swap bikes and have them available when needed.

9. CREW SCHEDULE AND ORGANIZATION

One of the biggest mistakes the RAAM racer can make is to do things erratically in the hope of optimizing sleep, crew movements, or any other aspects of the race at any given instant in time. Erratic sleep schedules and erratic crew movements are likely to lead to problems down the road. Instead, take a global view of the race, and focus on the **5 keystones**, with the ones pertaining to the crew schedule and organization in *ITALICS*:

1. Regular sleep, about 4 hours per day at about the same time each day.
2. Sleep in the middle of the day, when it is hottest.
3. Race uninterrupted through afternoon, night and morning.
4. *Make use of 2 stationary crew exchanges for racer hygiene breaks.*
5. *2 crew members in 3 vehicles keeps crews busy yet rested.*

Small concessions to keep things simple can make up an enormous amount of time down the road. Therefore, a more successful approach is to plan for the race flow to be simple, even if that means being only near-optimal at any given instant in time. The principle of global optimization being superior to local optimization is important in many fields of engineering and science, and can be used equally to "engineer" a successful solo RAAM.

This principle is nowhere more important than when planning the crew's movements and the overall race flow. The standard approach often involves up to 10 crew members, shuttle vehicles in addition to crew vehicles, RVs, three crew per vehicle while crewing the racer, and many other unnecessary, or even detrimental, complications. We advocate a simpler approach: three identical follow vehicles with two crew members in each, a fresh driver for the night crew (Crew #2) available mid-race, and a linear race flow where each crew has specific tasks that repeat every day. During the Honey Badger's 2016 race, his crew got better and smoother, instead of more tired and more inefficient, as the race progressed. Because every hour counts, an RV with shower/bed for the racer only can be added if the budget permits and can also house the spare crew member for Crew #2.

Table 9.1 illustrates the daily routine. Our solo RAAM strategy has the racer sleep in the early afternoon to avoid the mid-day heat, and to divide the daytime riding into two short halves. The three crews follow the racer from *ca* 16:30 to 23:00 (Crew #1), 23:00 to 05:30 (Crew #2), and 05:30 to 12:00 (Crew #3) race time, which is Eastern Daylight Savings Time. The exceptions on the first and last race day are described in Chapter 11. Note that many of the time blocks have flexibility built in. For example, Crew #2 could go to bed at 06:00 instead of 08:00, and do more driving in the afternoon, instead of splitting the catch-up drive into two halves.

Table 9.1. Representative daily crew schedule. Time blocks during which crews are following the racer are shown in yellow, sleep blocks are shown in blue.

Time (EDT)	Nom. miles	Racer schedule	Crew #1 schedule	Crew #2 schedule	Crew #3 schedule
12:00	Sleep	Sleep break: shower, hygiene, meal. Crew #1 wakes up racer	Drive ca. 200 miles to racer's motel	Sleep 08:00 to 16:00	Settle racer, run errands
13:00	Sleep				Drive ca. 200 miles to motel near morning shift takeover point
14:00	Sleep				
15:00	Sleep		Get racer ready		
16:00	0	Evening shift racing	Evening crew shift 1	Eat, shop	
17:00	16	Ride		Drive ca. 125 miles forward	
18:00	32	Ride			Errands
19:00	48	Ride			
20:00	64	Ride		Errands	Dinner, wind down
21:00	80	Ride			Sleep 21:00 to 04:00
22:00	95	Ride		Prep crew exch.	
23:00	112	Night shift racing	Drive to near motel	Night crew shift 2	
00:00	128	Ride	Eat, wind down		
01:00	144	Ride	Sleep 01:00 to 09:00		
02:00	160	Ride			
03:00	176	Ride			
04:00	192	Ride			
05:00	208	Ride			Prep crew exch.
06:00	224	Morning shift racing		Drive ca. 75 miles forward	Morning crew shift 3
07:00	240	Ride			
08:00	256	Ride		Sleep 08:00 to 16:00	
09:00	271	Ride	Errands		
10:00	285	Ride			
11:00	300	Ride	Drive to racer's motel		

To avoid fatigue, it is important to have three crews with 6- to 7-hour long shifts. This allows each crew 6 to 8 hours of sleep every day, while leaving time for errands, and for the ca. 200-mile drive required to catch up with the racer. Three fully equipped crew vehicles sanctioned during pre-race inspection also have the advantage that in an unforeseen incident, two vehicles are still available to follow the racer. We also tested 2 vs. 3 crew members per vehicle

(Chapter 6) and found 2 to be preferable. The navigator-feeder task can be combined into one without any loss of efficiency. The 3 van/2 crew scheme keeps the two crew members in each vehicle very busy, but makes the shifts shorter and sleep breaks longer. Both of these are good for morale and crew efficiency. An idle crew that gets little sleep is of no advantage to the racer.

Crew #1 has the task of awakening the racer on time each afternoon. We found the following approach to work best:

- Crew #1 arrives at the motel at least an hour before the racer needs to wake up. While driving there, they confirm with Crew #3 the requested wake-up time, as well as any bike swaps that are required.
- Crew #1 lays out the racer's fresh kit from their black clothing crate, organizes hygiene items from the racer's backpack, exchanges the bike left by Crew #3 for their bike if the day's riding requires it, and loads the red crates from the racer's room into their van.
- At the requested wake-up time (typically 3.75 hours after Crew #3 leaves the racer), Crew #1 starts making noise while doing their work in the racer's room. If the racer has not awakened after 15 minutes (4 hours total), the crew wakes up the racer.

As discussed in Chapter 5, this method works well because the REM cycle is roughly 90 minutes long, and a Masters racer needs plenty of deep sleep to recover sufficiently to handle 19+ hours of riding per day. Adding 0.5 hours to fall asleep in the Honey Badger's case, and 3 hours for 2 REM cycles, 3.75 hours is just a bit longer. That sleep duration facilitated spontaneous wake-up of our racer on most days, while the crew was rustling around the motel room to get things ready.

Photo 9.1 One crew member after collecting the old bottle during leapfrog (left), and the second crew member handing off the fresh bottle (right).

After waking up, the racer performs morning hygiene (Chapter 8) and gets dressed (about 10 minutes), then eats breakfast (about 5 minutes). While the racer gets ready, the crew organizes everything in the vehicle, turns in room keys, and finishes other tasks (*e.g.* check that the amber flashing lights and magnetic slow vehicle triangle are on). With a well-trained crew, the racer can be on the road about 15-20 minutes after getting out of bed.

Crew #1 remains in leap-frog mode from late afternoon to 19:00 local time. In leapfrog mode, we found it useful to hand off partial water bottles every 15 minutes in the desert heat (photo on page 85). A half bottle with ice remained cool for up to two 15-minute drink intervals. The empty bottle was collected by one crew member as the racer approached, and the full bottle was handed off by the second crew member while the racer continued riding. A salt capsule and a bar or gel every hour completed the food. The crew also shopped for a sandwich, which was generally fed to the racer form the car window during the last hour of the crew shift.

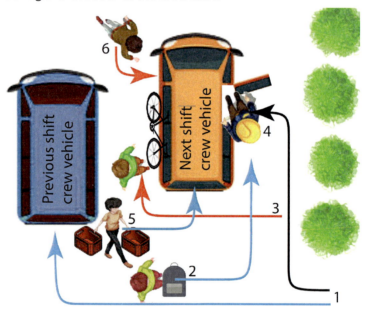

Figure 9.1. A typical crew exchange. (1) Racer (black arrows) arrives with the previous crew (blue arrows), and proceeds to the new crew's vehicle. A previous crew member (2) takes the hygiene backpack to the racer and new car, and helps him or her change. A new crew member (3) grabs the bike from the racer and preps it. The racer performs hygiene (4), including kit change, if needed. The other previous crew member (5) ferries the red crates to the new crew vehicle. A member of the new crew (6) is on call for small errands, and responsible for a final check of crates, backpack and RAAM GPS transfer (if jersey was changed). The racer can be back on the bike in under 10 minutes; a crew change is done every 6.5 hours, so it costs about 0.4 mph.

The two crew exchanges each day are done exclusively in stationary mode, as they occur around 23:00 from Crew #1 to Crew #2, and around 06:00 from

Crew #2 to Crew #3. The crew exchange is illustrated in Figure 9.1, and it is handled in the same way throughout the race for all crews. The fastest exchanges that we achieved were under 5 minutes long. The next crew either passes the racer and drives ahead, or is already ahead from their motel stay (Table 8.1). They then call or text the previous crew to provide the exchange location, usually accompanied by a road-side photo of the location. When cell service is not available, the relief crew positions itself very prominently near the road near a previously agreed-upon exchange point (about 100 miles into the previous crew's shift) and waves, made more visible by their reflective vests and ankle bands.

As illustrated in Figure 9.1, the crew members have designated tasks at the exchange to speed up the process: (2) The racer's soigneur brings the hygiene backpack to the racer and stands guard, helps with clothing changes, makes sure the jersey is restocked with gel and protein/salt source (300 mg sodium/80 mg potassium salt caps or beef jerky for the Honey Badger), and (if kit is changed) makes sure the new jersey has the RAAM GPS and emergency plastic bag in the middle pocket. (3) The bike wrangler grabs the bike from the racer, and preps it: puts on bottles as needed, checks brakes, (if the bike is swapped) transfers the smartphone and battery from the previous bike (or from the racer), and turns on the lights. (5) The carrier moves the red special clothes and tool crates (see Chapter 7) to the next vehicle, and hands the soigneur (2) any special clothes the racer requests from the red tool crate. (6) The supervisor runs small errands (*e.g.* fetches bottles or tools for the bike wrangler) and makes sure all vehicle tasks (*e.g.* turning on amber flashers, emergency flashers, and mounting the magnetic rear triangle on the next follow vehicle) are complete before getting in the next shift's vehicle and waiting for the racer to be on the way.

Crew #2 takes over after the first crew exchange around 23:00 to 01:00 depending on the time zone. Since this exchange takes place at night, gas stations are very convenient locations because of the lighting. If a gas station is not nearby, the headlights and flashlights (in the black milk crate) can also provide adequate lighting. Crew #2 operates purely in follow mode all night, pulling up next to the racer every 15 minutes (4x per hour) to check that he is hydrating regularly, providing the racer with a fresh bottle every hour and an occasional energy bar, and feeding the racer a sandwich near the end of the shift. A full bottle, instead of a half ice-cold bottle, can be handed to the racer during the cooler night shift. Crew #2 is the most likely the one that doses the racer with caffeine for the first time during the race (see Chapter 8 for dosage schedule). Crew #2 should start the caffeine treatment as late as possible during the race (Day 7 or later), to avoid racer acclimatization.

Crew #2 has the most monotonous drive. The two crew members are encouraged to jet-lag themselves like the racer, and sleep from 08:00 to 16:00. Due to work obligations prior to the race, the Crew #2 members may not be able to fully jet-lag. For this reason, a relief driver is provided as a 7th crew member. Ideally, the relief driver joins Crew #2 (or swaps with one of the members of Crew #2), shortly after the racer crosses the Mississippi, around Day 7. By then, Crew #2 will feel very tired if they have been unable to sleep adequately during the day. During RAAM 2016, we added a crew member at Effingham, TS 37. This made the task of Crew #2 much easier, and usually allowed one of its members to nod off in the car while the other two were handling the driving and navigator/feeder tasks.

Crew #2 may need to rotate tasks once or twice per night, which requires a brief stop to be safe (e.g. for driver exchange). These rotations should also be used for restroom breaks, to avoid wasting more than 2 minutes every few hours. The crew generally cannot wait 6 to 7 hours for the next exchange to use a restroom, and using containers in the car is a recipe for disaster. The racer should follow the same schedule, and not urinate on the bike. Although this may be done during shorter races (e.g. Ironman), the irritation in the seating area from even just a few drops of liquid gone astray, the cleaning of the bike, and other such pitfalls make it worthwhile for everyone to stop briefly.

Crew #3 takes over in another stationary exchange like the one shown in Figure 9.1 (night mode stops at 09:00 according to the 2016 rules). Like Crew #1, Crew #3 can sleep at night and gets to see some scenery while driving, so their task is not as monotonous as Crew #2's. After 09:00, Crew #3 generally goes into leapfrog mode, unless the race is passing through an Indian reservation, or truly busy roads demand follow mode to protect the racer. The feeding proceeds as with Crew #1.

Crew #3 is responsible for putting the racer to bed. The timing of this is important, so the racer sleeps in the middle of the day and splits the hot hours of the day in half. It is also important so that the racer does not become too fatigued. During the 2016 race, the team lapsed only once (Day 4) and let the racer go to rest too late. The Honey Badger did not fall asleep that evening (strong circadian rhythm), and had to ride a shorter day (about 200 miles instead of 280-320 miles) the following day to get back on the mid-day schedule. Such a lapse, most likely caused by unavailability of a convenient motel, or a dangerous desire to stay on a pre-conceived schedule when there are delays, can be avoided if an RV is rented for the racer to shower and sleep in. However, the extra cost of $6000 or so (RV rental, gas, an extra RV crew member, who also drives the spare crew member for Crew #2) may not be worth it to some racers, although it is likely to save several hours off the finish time (Chapter 11).

When putting the racer to rest, efficiency is important. Crew #3 should alert hotel staff about 1 hour before arrival so they will turn the air conditioning on in the room. In some desert motels, it can get extremely hot in an unoccupied room. Upon arrival at the motel, one member of Crew #3 takes the racer and hygiene bag to the room, double-checks the air conditioning, and then gets the racer's bedtime food. We had someone with a medical background on Crew #3, and he had a quick discussion with the racer every day. The other crew member brings the two red crates and the bike (to be ridden or exchanged with Crew #1) into the room, inventories and re-organizes the crates, and preps the bike (turns lights off, cleans, and does a quick mechanical check). All this happens in about 15 minutes while the racer showers, does hygiene and eats "dinner," and then Crew #3 draws the curtains and the racer goes to bed. Crew #3 then informs motel staff about who Crew #1 is, and to hand the next crew the racer's room key when they arrive. Some motels will (correctly so) get very suspicious if two people come in unannounced and want to get the key to one of the guest's rooms.

This crew #1-crew#2-crew#3 cycle repeats every day, and in the racer's experience, becomes second-nature to the crew by the third day. There is no reason to worry that the crew will get bored. Shopping for the racer's food cravings, fixing problems with bikes, doing a little sight-seeing when there is time, running emergency errands (like buying winter gloves for a cold descent when the racer had forgotten to pack his), and many other such things will keep all three crews busy while they are not sleeping or following the racer.

Some other do's and don'ts for the crews:
- If you spray your racer for cooling during the day, don't overdo it. If (s)he gets wet between the legs, the resulting chafing will quickly end the race.
- Do not wet/ice the racer's feet: it can cause blistering, which will end the race. With our race strategy of only a few hours at a time in the heat of the day, hot feet are less of an issue. Make sure to have oversize shoes on during the hot daytime.

- If your racer has a wet chamois from sweat or other liquids, change the shorts or bibs immediately. As a rule, they should be changed for sure at the end of the first (day) shift; a change may not be necessary for the night shift change.
- If you put ice on your racer in places that can drip into the shorts, put the ice in a zip-loc bag and seal. On the neck, an ice pouch that slowly releases cold water is generally OK, but make sure to re-apply sunscreen when it is removed.
- Store sandwiches in a zip-loc bag in the cooler, to avoid the racer's food getting soggy.
- A helmet with a white towel hanging over the neck and tucked into the top of the jersey is very handy for spraying to keep the neck cool. Again, apply sunscreen when it is removed.
- When the temperature is above 80 °F (27 °C), consider switching between two helmets, and storing one in an ice cooler while the other is in use. A cool helmet will feel good when your racer gets back on the road if a short break was necessary.
- Crews #1 and #3 should inventory, and if necessary, organize the red crates every single day while the racer is sleeping.
- Wash the racer's used clothes with plenty of soap, and make sure the shorts are completely dried before use to avoid chafing and saddle sores. Most hotels have a hair drier to accelerate the process.
- If your racer is forgetful about regular drinking, agree on a signal (e.g. ring a cow bell) about every 15 minutes for a 1/4 bottle drink. However, if your racer waves you off, don't insist. Overdrinking and hyponatremia can also be big problems.
- Bike bottles don't need washing for every refill during the shift, but to avoid mold, do wash with soap all your bottles after each shift.
- Elicit a regular thumbs-up or OK-sign from your racer when you pass during leapfrog. Make full use of the 4x per hour allowance during follow mode to drive up next to your racer and check. This gives you feedback that your racer is not having problems.
- Leapfrog your racer from behind: let them pass, and when they are out of sight, get going, pass, and park again. You should never be far ahead of your racer. The only exception is if you need to stop at a gas station. If you do, make sure a crew member remains near the road to watch for the racer. Do not trust GPS info, it can be delayed – NEVER TAKE YOUR EYES OFF THE ROAD and allow your racer to pass you unbeknownst to you.
- If it's very hot and your racer starts arguing, or becomes unresponsive, stop your racer, remove the helmet, and douse cold water over his or her head without any discussion. Be sure not to get the shorts wet while you do so. A dousing, and 5-10 minutes' rest in the air-conditioned car, will usually return the racer to common sense. Do not let a racer with signs of heat exhaustion make any decision until these two steps have been taken.

One additional task for the crew is to keep constant track of other Masters racers. However, the Honey Badger's crew was explicitly told not to inform him about the competitors' progress until the end of Day 7, and they kept to it. The reason is that the true favorites in the Masters category are not likely to emerge until then. The solo Masters racers are all very experienced, and tend to have strong, but rarely world class, power output. (Why? Having tasted Tour-level racing, world class racers have a tendency to retire once their power is reduced by age, and so they rarely race as Masters. However, the university professors, doctors, or camp counselors who are doing this as a hobby, are very likely to be among the top riders of their amateur club at home.) Early on, there is no reason for a racer to go faster than the HR = 160-age formula allows, or to sleep much less than 4 hours. Otherwise, he/she will simply fall behind later in the race. If you are at the back of the pack by Day 8, it is not likely that you will pass the frontrunner, unless they really overexerted themselves early on. However, if you are in the middle or towards the front of the pack by Day 8, you have a real chance of ending up on the podium. If you manage your heart rate and sleep carefully for the first 7 days, you will see that other racers, who sleep to little or too irregularly, will begin to slow down considerably. Someone experienced with data analysis (e.g. running averages, short term linear extrapolation) can be very useful on your crew after Day 7. We had Greg Scott crunch numbers in real time to estimate who was falling back and who was still a threat. As seen in Figure 3.11, the GPS data available nowadays during the race makes it easy to estimate trends during the race. This trend data is updated in real time at the RAAM website now that race management is using a small GPS unit on the racer.

This chapter would be incomplete without mentioning one of the most important elements that keeps your crew on track during solo RAAM: the route book. You get three hardcopies from race management before the start, perfect for a 3-crew strategy. In addition, the book is available online at least a month before the race. We used the early version to revise the RideWithGPS maps before the race, so it would follow the route book exactly.

Figure 9.2 shows a well-used page from the 2016 route book. At the top of each page, the book summarizes the route, any challenges, and rules to pay attention to during the upcoming stretch (*e.g.* follow-mode-only in an Indian reservation). Each page guides you from one time station to the next. The crew on duty should synch their vehicle odometer with the route book. When crew exchanges occur between time stations, the next crew should make sure to note where they are in the route book, so they can add to the odometer reading accordingly. The route book provides very clear directions, often with landmarks to help. These tend to be absent from the GPS, so the navigator should keep an eye on the route book at all times, even if GPS is used as the primary means of navigation.

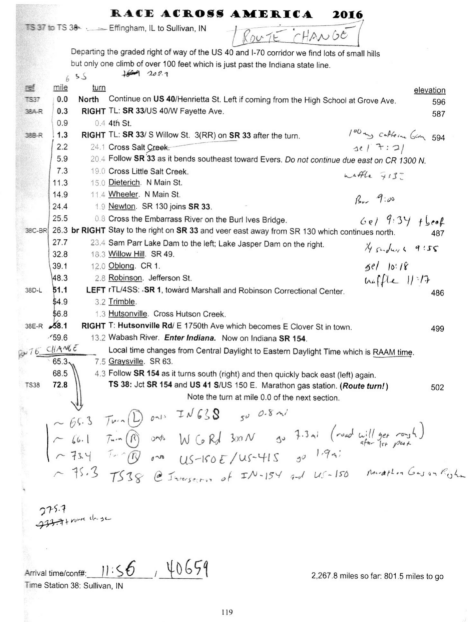

Figure 9.2. A page from the RAAM route book (reproduced with permission).

Route changes may be announced by race headquarters during the race, and in such situations the crew has to guide the racer if there is no time to update the racer's GPS with voice commands (*e.g.* from RideWithGPS). The sample page shows a route change noted between TS 37 and 38. Route changes are never good, and this one was onto a quiet but extremely rough road, where the pavement had decayed to coarse gravel texture.

The navigator-feeder also noted the times of gels, half sandwiches, and the like on the right side, to keep track of proper nutrition for the racer. At the bottom, the arrival time at TS 38 was noted, along with the confirmation number the crew receives when calling the TS in to race headquarters. Well-kept route books returned to the racer by each crew at the end of RAAM also make it easy to reconstruct race details that the racer may not remember.

It was important for the crew to be trained with the route book during the practice race (Chapter 6), even though we had to use an older version of the route book. During the real race, however, the crew rarely had to give the racer directions because he had his own GPS and entertainment system through the right earbud. When this failed (*e.g.* the route change at mile 65.3 in Figure 9.2), we used a simple auditory system, rather than mounting loudspeakers on the crew vehicles to blare commands or music. A short honk meant that the crew was about to signal the racer (to distinguish it from the long honk of a passing car). Directions were given using the vehicle's horn as follows:

- Short – long = STOP
- Short – short = right turn
- Short – short – short = left turn

We picked these signals because they mimic the audio cues from RideWithGPS, the cycling mapping and navigation software we used. Thus, they were easy for everyone to remember. The first signal was most often used in follow mode when a caravan was threatening to build up behind the crew vehicle. In that case, the racer would stop as soon as it was safely possible and it looked like the crew vehicle could also get off the road to let traffic pass. During follow mode, under no circumstances can the racer keep going when the crew vehicle stops to allow traffic to pass.

In addition to signaling directions, the crew did some additional racer conditioning, such as ringing a bell every 15 minutes in follow mode to remind the racer to drink (and ring again when he failed to do so). It felt quite Pavlovian after a few days, but it did the job of avoiding unnecessary driving of the crew next to the racer in follow mode, which was particularly helpful in heavier traffic.

10. DEALING WITH THE ELEMENTS

In this chapter, we briefly discuss how to deal with the elements, which include weather, accidents, illness, and other predictable or unpredictable difficulties.

One of the "elements" is darkness. Our race strategy requires riding in the dark, typically from 21:00 to 05:00, or at least 8 hours each race day. It is very important that both the racer and the crew are trained to handle it. For the racer, this means at least 500 miles a month of night riding in the year before the race, as well as practice races that involve night riding, such as the two-man team RAAM, or a long randonnée like Paris-Brest-Paris. It is simply a matter of getting used to riding fast in limited lighting conditions, and not being lulled into a false sense of speed by the quiet, tunnel-like riding at night. Crew training is also very important. Driving 10 meters behind a cyclist at 40 miles per hour on a descent, while steering through curves to provide maximum illumination from the follow vehicle high-beam, is not part of any driver's education. The crew has to learn this during the practice race, and during some practice riding in the dark before the race start in Oceanside. It helps to have three crews split the job, reducing crew fatigue and making precise driving easier. It will take the crew hours of practice until they can stick right behind the racer at night. Every crew member should go through it, even if they are more likely to act as navigator/feeder. It is particularly important for the night crew (Crew #2); Jay Yost, Roy Tylinski, and crew chief Harry Zink were all adept at driving closely behind the racer with the high beams on when no oncoming traffic was present. A crew skilled at night driving can save hours over the duration of the race, by enabling the cyclist to maintain a higher speed with confidence despite potholes or gravel patches on the road.

Another element is storms. The weather in the mountains, but also from Kansas to Maryland, can bring powerful storms. The Honey Badger had to suffer through two of them. One was just a rain storm, inconveniently timed during steep descents in the Appalachians. The racer simply rode though these, taking care not to corner too hard on the descents. The rain clothing discussed in Chapter 7 is completely sufficient to deal with this problem. Unless the temperature fell below 50 °F, a yellow O2 rain jacket, a helmet cover, plastic shorts (covering the bib shorts), and supermarket bags as booties were sufficient. The booties deserve special mention. After a lot of testing, Martin concluded that no commercial shoe covers actually work in the rain: at the very least, the cleat opening eventually lets in water after 15 minutes in a strong rain. So instead, the Honey Badger used a thin supermarket plastic bag wrapped around his shoes and legs, taped to the shaved legs with duct tape to prevent rain from seeping down into the shoes. With the right pedals (the Honey Badger used Speedplay Frog touring pedals, which engage the cleat in a manner non-destructive to a thin plastic bag), this method provides a 100% seal against cold rain. A new pair of bags was simply used for each storm. Additional items that help in wet conditions: an attachable rear fender reduces the spray onto the bib shorts which helps avoid chafing; and extra pairs of shoes are absolutely necessary. That way, shoes can be allowed to get wet in a mild or warm rain that lasts for <2 hours, where clothing changes are not really worth the time lost. The crew may want to lubricate the racer's feet with Vaseline or RunGoo between the toes and on the ball of the foot if rain is predicted, to avoid blisters from chafing in wet shoes and socks. During a severe thunderstorm in Ohio, we simply had to sit out an hour in the follow vehicle (see photo in Chapter 12). The time was not entirely wasted: the racer somehow managed to sleep soundly for about a half hour despite the thunder and lighting, and that time was deducted from the next sleep cycle (3h 30m instead of 4h) without any ill effects.

Wind also causes many problems. In 2016, headwinds blew in eastern Colorado and Kansas, as well as in Maryland. Fortunately, no 40 mph crosswinds materialized in Kansas, but this does happen frequently during RAAM. For this reason, we carried low profile rims, to replace the tri-spokes on the Superbike and the deep rims on the TCR0 (Chapter 7). Each vehicle had a set of front/rear replacement wheels along with a bike. There is no substitute for training in wind. Martin endlessly trained in 15 mph winds for 1000s of miles in the flatlands of Illinois, getting used to the constant push required when there are no trees or buildings to provide shelter. We strongly recommend purposeful training against headwinds, with at least a long ride every week that includes 4+ hours of strong headwind. An excellent time trial bike is also important. The Dimond Superbike (Chapter 7) offered better comfort (thanks to the beam geometry) and aerodynamics (thanks to many wide airfoil shapes) than Martin's other, UCI-legal, time trial bike. Riding a fast time trial bike that is also comfortable in an aggressive position for 19 to 21 hours non-stop was key to the catch-up strategy, which brought the Honey Badger from 100 miles behind in Colorado to 100 miles ahead in Missouri despite the cross- and headwinds. In eastern Colorado, cross- and headwinds reached over 15 mph many times. The rider and crew need plenty of practice to handle and tolerate following a racer who is being swept several feet left and right by cross winds. Such sweeping is unavoidable if the racer maintains a relaxed grip on the bike, which is key to avoid riding fatigue on a high cross-section frame and wheelset in a crosswind.

Descents are another issue that the crew and rider must deal with, whether it is at night (see above) or during the rain. It is very important that the racer extensively practice descending under challenging conditions, so it can be done safely yet rapidly. The Honey Badger went out of his way to train and race in California, Arizona, Colorado and other hilly places in the three years before the race, to make sure he could do 40 mph descents consistently and without pushing the limits of his bike handling in any way. The key during the race is to avoid pushing the bike handling limits that were learned before the race. The temptation can be strong in the heat of the moment. Certainly a few minutes could be eked out by aggressive riding, but the potential cost is too high: a crash in the Appalachians, when the rider is fatigued and not at his or her best, can spell a late but abrupt end to a heretofore successful race. We had a crash on our 2013 two-man team RAAM on a gravelly stretch at night. It almost spelled the end of the race for one racer, but could have been avoided by more conservative riding.

Accidents and delays can happen, and the Honey Badger's crew had to deal with both of these during the race. Fortunately, the crew was able to deal with a vehicle accident during the race without alerting the racer, so his concentration was not interrupted by a lot of worrying. As an aside, making sure all of your vehicles and drivers are well-insured is wise. Likewise, when one crew slept in and was late for their crew exchange, this did not turn into a problem for the racer either. Having three equivalent follow vehicles available is an important element of any strategy dealing with accidents and delays. It provides redundancy so the racer never has to wait, and the crews are rested enough so that if a contingency arises and one of the crews has to accompany the racer for a few hours longer, they are not overly fatigued by the time the problem is resolved. There are also delays that do not cost any time: We once waited for 20 minutes for a parade that blocked the crew vehicle from passing during follow support. Such delays can be called in to race headquarters, who can verify them with their GPS unit and provide a time credit.

Bicycle mechanical problems are another "element" that will almost invariably arise. First, the racer provided training for the most common tasks (e.g. changing a tube, adjusting brakes) to all crew attending the practice race

(Chapter 6). The tool crates in Chapter 7 provide the means of fixing most problems. Having four bikes along provides plenty of reserves. The Honey Badger had two crew members experienced with bicycle mechanics (Roy Tylinski and Greg Scott). Roy, in particular, was adept at fixing complex shifter or brake problems on the fly while the crew vehicle was driving. Roy also provided additional training for the crew in the two days before the race start in Oceanside. As with all other problems, having three crews who can do shopping and meet each other at various times of the day makes it easy to swap bikes, obtain parts, and distribute them so they can be installed. During the entire 2016 RAAM, the racer had to use his second-choice bike only once for a total of about 3 hours. The situation arose because the set of spare wheels in one of the vans did not fit the narrower brake profile of the bike of choice after a flat. The real moral of that story is that the racer or a designated crew member needs to check every combination of wheel and bike before the race, if they are indeed going to be used interchangeably.

Racer illness or injury is another unpredictable "element." Having a member of the crew certified in First Aid through an organization like the Red Cross could be invaluable to deal with both emergent issues as well as minor injuries. Our crew member Dr. Ed Scott provided practical first-aid advice, kept an eye on Martin's red eye and blistered foot, and volunteered to take care of pharmacy trips. Having someone with medical experience on the crew provided mental peace of mind to the racer, just in case there might be a real emergency. Ed also provided ice packs for the knees, and other assorted advice for small ills and pains that came up. At the beginning of RAAM, Martin was finishing a course of antibiotics prescribed by his primary care physician (for a bike crash and elbow injury that occurred just before the race, and left some debris in his elbow). The lacerated elbow made it harder to ride on the aerobars, but as a silver lining on the cloud of the injury, Martin may have had some extra immunity to bacterial infection during the first few days of the race. It is wise for the crew to have a line of communication with the racer's primary care physician and full access to health insurance information in case any serious medical issues were to arise.

It must be said again here that the best prevention for racer illness due to immune system failure, for racer fidgeting (see Chapter 8), or worse, for racer hallucinations, temper tantrums or other mental aberrations, is sufficient and regular sleep (**keystones 1 and 2**). Leg fatigue has almost nothing to do with such problems, or with slow riding in general. With hygiene under control, lack of sleep is the only important cause of problems (Chapter 3) later in the race, while overheating is the main cause at the start of the race (see tips on page 107/108). Our four-hour sleep strategy during the day provided enough sleep, and not once during the race did the Honey Badger lose his temper, threaten to stop racing, or do anything worse than fidget a bit during the last race day, when the sit bone pain and cumulative effects of chafing became significant. It is important that you determine your need for sleep using long practice races such as two-man team RAAM, P-B-P, or three-day sequences of practice rides with little sleep, while monitoring your ability to sustain 160-age heart rate during the final stages of these races and training sequences (Chapter 5). The long-sleep during-daytime strategy enables on-bike racing speeds similar to the Open male winners, finishing times in line with the top Masters racers, but without the ill side effects of complete sleep deprivation. The exception is on the final race day, when a sleep cycle may be skipped to stay at the head of the race.

During the 2016 race, some prominent and very strong racers abandoned over small problems. Riding at the front of the race the whole way, they had suffered significant sleep deprivation. Stick to the strategy in this book, and you will never look for the non-existent Chapter on how the crew should deal with a hallucinating or aggressive racer. Instead, you will work your way towards the front of the Masters race by the time you cross the Mississippi.

11. START AND ENDGAME

The beginning of any race almost always falls outside of the routine because the racer is stuck with the race start time determined by the race organizers. In our case, the race start at 13:00 west coast time fell right in the middle of the preferred mid-day sleep period for the racer. We dealt with this by making day one a somewhat longer day, sustainable because the racer is still fresh on Day 1, and by gradually shifting the sleeping time from 10:00– 14:00 (day one in CA) to 14:00 – 18:00 (Day 9 in Ohio). Before the race, the racer (who usually sleeps about 7 hours/day) jetlagged himself to sleep from about 04:00 to 11:00 CA time. Thus it was easy to get up after 10:00 on race day, eat, get dressed and be ready at the start by noon when the first teams left. We then raced until about 10:00 the following day (reaching Salome about 342 miles down the road). This was early enough to overlap with the end of Martin's jet lagged sleep period, and so he was able to sleep for about 4 hours. From then on, the sleep schedule was slowly ramped forward, in synch with the one-hour time zone transitions as we moved east. So a sleep of 14:00-18:00 in Ohio was actually still the same as 11:00-15:00 in California.

The Honey Badger provided his crew with a fairly detailed time table for the first two days, for two reasons: It clarified how the first day would differ from the normal routine discussed in Chapter 8. It also provided the crew with some welcome guidance during the first couple of days, when they were fresh on the job, and the normal routine had not yet been established. We highly recommend providing such a document to the crew, and we reproduce it here (in italics):

Projected schedule at start:

June 14th, 2016: (all times PDT time zone)

11:00 Julie wakes up Martin (good practice for Crew #1, the wake-up crew); racing kit from her crew's black box is laid out & breakfast is ready.

11:45 Martin arrives with bike at start line. Crew #3, Greg & Ed, will be in the start line van.

13:00 Martin starts race on the Dimond superbike; Greg and Ed drive off to their first hotel ca. 230 miles out (The Blythe Super 8 @ (760) 922-8881 has better rating than Days Inn @ (760) 922-5101)

13:15 Crew #1, Julie & Lana, drive to the leapfrog start (Old Castle Trading Post on Old Castle Road), using the directions for vehicles from the route book: 16 miles by the bypass route. Position yourselves prominently near the road to save time, and have a crew member on the lookout. Have the Merlin bike out of your vehicle, lights on and ready to go with a half-filled ice-drink bottle.

12:45 Crew #2, Harry and Roy, get up (house lease ends at 1 PM). They have the day off in Oceanside, but need to be at rendezvous with Julie & Lana ca. 125 miles down the road (Elmore Desert Ranch) by 19:00.

14:15 After 23 miles of racing, Martin meets Crew #1 at Old Castle site, switches from Dimond to Merlin bike (climbing and glass elevator descent coming up). Front and rear lights on and half-filled ice-drink bottle. Martin only has to move the iPhone+battery cover. This is where Crew #1 starts obligatory daytime leapfrog.

17:30 Martin and Crew #1 pass Time Station TS 01 in Lake Henshaw.

19:00 Follow mode starts, but Crew #1 put the slow vehicle sign on and turned the lights on at Old Castle Road already, no need to stop.

20:45 Martin and Crew #1 reach ca. mile 125 near Elmore Desert Ranch, where Crew #2, Harry & Roy, have alerted crew 1 by cell phone where they are waiting; Crew #2 takes over in a stationary crew exchange. Crew #1 drives forward partway (e.g. Quality Inn, Parker AZ @ (928) 669-2133) to their motel to get some sleep.

21:30 Martin and Crew #2 pass TS 02 in Brawley.

June 15th (all times PDT time zone):

03:20 Martin & Crew #2 reach Blythe, where Crew #3, Greg & Ed, got up bright and early and do a stationary crew exchange at or near their hotel, after letting Crew #2 know where. Crew #2 drives forward as far as possible before going to bed at their hotel. (at least 90-120 miles is suggested; for example The Westward Motel in Salome @ (208) 610-3516 or Sheffler's motel in Salome @ (928) 859-3001).

06:15 Martin and Crew #3 pass TS 04 in Parker, AZ

09:00 Leapfrog mode starts somewhere past Parker AZ, no need to stop, just drive past Martin and wave so he knows.

10:15 Martin and Crew #3 reach Salome AZ, where Martin goes to bed for his first sleep cycle. Crew #3 leaves the two red boxes, the superbike and Martins' backpack in his room, and sets up "dinner." Make sure the RAAM GPS is with the racer. Crew #3 then drives ca. 210 miles ahead to their own motel (Camp

Verde AZ Days Inn, Super 8, or Comfort Inn). Martin should <u>not stop any later than 10:30 AM</u> to avoid fatigue early on. Better to do fewer miles to Bouse (still over 300) on Day 1, if Salome looks unreachable by 10:30 AM.

14:45 Crew #1 wakes up Martin: Julie & Lana have driven from Parker and got to Salome by 13:45, about an hour ahead of waking up Martin. They laid out Martin's fresh kit from their black clothes box, and have "breakfast" set up. Note that Martin gets ca. 3.5 to 4 h sleep during a 4.5-hour rest stop: 0.5 to 1 hour is spent showering, doing hygiene, eating dinner, and in the afternoon getting dressed and eating breakfast.

18:45 Martin and Crew #1 pass TS 06 in Congress AZ.

19:00 Follow mode starts for Crew #1. By now, Crew # 2 are up and driving the rest of the way towards the rendezvous before Prescott, AZ around mile 440 into the race.

22:30 Martin and Crew #1 pass TS 07 in Prescott AZ

23:45 Martin and Crew #1 arrive at the rendezvous past Prescott, and Crew #2 takes over. Crew #1 drives to Camp Verde and goes to sleep at the motel they reserved by around 01:00 on June 16th. They will drive the remainder of their 210 miles to the next rendezvous in the late morning.

June 16th (all times PDT time zone):

07:15 Crew #3 takes over from Crew #2 just past 7 AM local time, after getting up at their hotel in Camp Verde at a slightly more civilized time of 5 AM.

You get the picture. From here on out, it becomes too hard to predict the optimal hotels for Martin (Crew #3 in charge) or for crews (each crew in charge of their own). But as a rule of thumb, Crew #1 should drive ahead a little and find a nearby motel, then do most of the 200-mile catch-up after getting up. Crew #2 can split their catch-up drive in two. And Crew #3 should drive ~200 miles ahead first and pick a motel right on the route if possible, to make exchange easy.

09:00 Leapfrog mode starts somewhere after Camp Verde around mile 530.

The crew found the above instruction sheet very useful during the first three days of the race. Note that we had to deviate from the 10-day schedule described in Chapter 8 after a couple more days, and move to the 11-day schedule. We were 4 hours behind schedule by the time we emerged from the Rocky Mountains in Trinidad, CO. With a tailwind in the central US, this could have been made up. Unfortunately, it had become clear from weather forecasts that a cross/headwind of up to 15 mph from the southeast was going to greet us, instead of the seasonal 10 mph SW wind. At least there was no 40 mph south wind in Kansas, also not unheard of during RAAM. Since the Honey Badger had fallen about 4 hours behind the 10-day sleep schedule, we needed to put in a shorter day to bring racer and crew back on schedule (**keystone 2 -** racer sleeps through the hottest middle part of the day, instead of in the early evening).

The end of the race also has to depart from the routine laid out in Chapters 8 and 9. First of all, even the Masters racer can tolerate a somewhat shorter sleep break one cycle from the end. Martin had tested this during Paris-Brest-Paris. So at the end of Day 10, when we had reached Oakland, MD, the Honey Badger skipped the 4-hour motel stop and slept for only 2 hours in the back of the Crew #3 van. At that point, the 2nd place Masters racer was about 85 miles (5.5 hours) behind, and so a shorter rest break seemed prudent. As we had anticipated, the one-time shorter break did not have a major effect on the next day's riding, which included 6 steep climbs in the Appalachians after TS 48 (Cumberland). Our racer made it through the climbs with good speed, comparable to his climbing in the Rockies and Ozarks. However, things deteriorated at the very end. We needed more than 24 hours to get from Oakland to the Annapolis finish line, and so a short sleep at the end of Day 10 was followed by no sleep on the afternoon of Day 11. After Mt. Airy, our racer became unable to push down the rollers fast enough to coast up the next one on the Superbike, and we had to transfer Martin over to the Merlin so he could slowly climb his way up hills. The average speed of 11 mph after Mt. Airy is the main factor that reduced the Day 11 average in Table 8.4 about 0.5 mph below the daily average of Day 2, a similar climbing day.

We still reached the official finish line about 9 hours ahead of the 2nd place rider, a clear margin. As discussed in Chapter 3, Martin ended up on the bike for 8.7 days, and off the bike for just over 2 days. This is to be compared with 8.6 days on, 1 day off for the top Open male racer, and 9.7 days on, 1.6 days off for the second Masters finisher. Clearly, the strategy of more sleep, and riding as fast as the top three Open male racers had paid off. Not only did it get our racer to the finish well ahead of the competition, after lagging behind during the first half of RAAM, but the Honey Badger arrived at the podium in good physical condition, jumping up onto the podium rather than taking the stairs, and staying up for the 1st award banquet despite not having slept at all for 28 hours on the last day of the race.

Martin did one last full hygiene routine between the official finish line and the parade finish, at a Shell gas station designated by RAAM headquarters. This also included wiping off his body with alcohol cleaning wipes, shaving, and changing into a completely fresh kit. Likewise, his bike was cleaned up by the crew mechanic before the final few miles. Then the racer on his bike and two of our crew vans were met by an escort vehicle that guided us to the parade finish. There, Martin waited for 2 or 3 minutes until a volunteer waved him into the chute to cross the finish line. The racer and crew gave a brief interview on the podium, and then headed off to the banquet with friends and family. Thus ended our 2016 RAAM effort.

Hindsight is 20/20, as the saying goes. After any race, there are things one would have done differently, and especially a very long race like RAAM is no exception. Here is a summary of the items (also discussed elsewhere in this book) that the racer and team would do differently the next time around.

1. Martin suffered from red-eye early in the race, with the first symptoms showing up in Arizona on Day 2 when riding through the desert to Yarnell. The irritation was most likely due to a combination of sandstorms and extreme dryness that we raced through. It might have been prevented by systematically taking eye drops from the start at every crew exchange. Our racer only started to do this on Day 3, when the symptoms had already become quite bad. Likewise, carefully washing out the eyes in the shower at each rest stop may have helped, if the irritation was due to sand in addition to dryness. The red-eye cleared up by Day 7 or so while taking eye drops 3 to 4 times a day, but may have been prevented altogether if our racer had used wrap-around goggles in the desert.

2. Martin also suffered hotfoot on the left foot, losing feeling in one of the small toes for several weeks after the race and building up an excessive callous on the ball of the foot. He used two pairs of shoes during the race. One had been worn during two-man team RAAM and Paris-Brest-Paris (1500 and 780 mile races, respectively). The other had been tested only for several thousand miles of training, with 90-100-220-130 mile consecutive days being typical long training segments. The training-only pair was responsible for the problem, which stopped worsening when Martin switched over to the well-worn pair completely a few days into the race. The conclusion is, wear only shoes that leave your feet in perfect shape after at least a 500+ mile race. Shoes that feel good after a bunch of 200-mile training rides could still cause a problem. Both pairs of shoes were made by the same manufacturer (Shimano) and were 2 sizes larger than Martin's normal streetwear (45 instead

of 43 Shimano size, which corresponds to 44/42 of typical European manufacturers since Shimano sizes on the small side). The soles of the two pairs were very similar, but the toe boxes had slightly different shapes.

3. We recommend a somewhat longer break than our racer took on the eve of the final day of solo RAAM, at a motel or in an RV. The Honey Badger rested for barely two hours in the back of a crew van in Oakland, MD, instead of the customary 4 hours at a motel. We wanted to make sure we kept a healthy separation to the 2nd place Masters racer. Two hours of sleep kept that separation at over 3.5 hours, but in hindsight, 2.5 hours of separation would have been enough, allowing a 3-hour sleep break at a motel in Oakland, rather than a 2-hour sleep in the van. The Honey Badger probably could have reclaimed that hour and more, by riding faster in the last 85 miles. The problem was that there were 25 hours of racing left after Oakland. Thus, the racer ended up with one half-length sleep period in Oakland, and one sleep period skipped entirely *ca.* 5 hours before the finish line. This combination of a short sleep break and a missed sleep break resulted in extreme fatigue and a very low heart rate (80 beats per minute) during the last 85 miles. Compared to a day with similar altitude gain earlier in the race, we lost 3.4 mph of speed because Martin rode more slowly and also stopped more frequently. A loss of 3.4 mph over 5 hours amounts to 17 miles, or an hour lost. Thus the 2-hour sleep break did not buy anything over a 3-hour sleep break, except some peace of mind at the beginning of the riding day. Of course, this is really a decision that has to be made by weighing racer speed, recovery, and positioning, and will be specific to every race.

4. Several times during RAAM, our racer slept at a motel just before a time station. While Martin felt good by calling in a time station before going to bed, we could have saved about an hour off the race total by going to the motel first when it lay ahead of the time station, rather than calling in our racer first and then ferrying him back to the motel.

5. Pre-race, it would have been helpful to rent the vehicles two days ahead of departure instead of one day. We ran into a problem with vehicle availability, and the rental company substituted an SUV for our requested mini-van. The vehicle worked out OK, but not as well as the mini-van. With an extra day, we could have insisted on delivery of the requested vehicle instead of making do with what was on hand due to our imminent departure.

6. Finally, if finances permit, and a comfortable RV with a bed and shower can be obtained, the reader might consider shower, hygiene and sleep breaks for

the racer in an RV instead of a motel. Crews (except the RV crew) would generally still stay at a motel. The main reason to get an RV for the racer is that RV stops can be configured at the optimal time each day with less than 30 minutes or so uncertainty, depending on availability of a good parking spot. Availability of motels caused our racer to shift his sleep break too late on the eve of Day 5, and this had to be corrected for with a shorter (195-mile) race day on Day 5. Likewise, an RV in Oakland, MD, would have allowed an efficient but still comfortable shorter sleep break before the last race day, as discussed in the third point above. Finally, at the end of Day 7 in Missouri, we could have saved a half hour by not going off the race route (US 50) to a motel in Owensville. The alternative would have been to forge ahead to Washington, MO, but this would again have resulted in too late a sleep break, and the correct choice was made to go a little off-route for an on-time sleep break. We estimate that having an RV available could have saved us about two hours on days 5/6, an hour on Day 7, and an hour on Day 10. All in all, we estimate that optimized sleep breaks (reduced fatigue) and time saved over the motel routine (driving time, dealing with motels) would have resulted in a 4-hour gain. That is a significant time savings in a close contest, to be weighed against major additional costs and logistical complications.

To summarize the advice of this chapter: Make sure the racer and Crew #2 are jet-lagged to sleep from *ca.* 04:00 to 11:00 CA time when they reach Oceanside (**keystone 2**); prepare a 2-day step-by-step summary of race flow for the crew to ease into their tasks; use eye drops 3 to 4 times a day from the race start, to avoid red-eye from the Arizona desert dryness and the altitude in the Rockies; trust only shoes you have worn for at least a 500+ mile race without any symptoms (and, as discussed elsewhere in the book, mount the cleats fairly far back); cut the last sleep break only by 1 hour, if you have several hours beyond the usual 19 to ride on the last day, or you will lose the hour to fatigue (**keystone 1**); if you use a motel for the racer's rest, resist the urge to pass and call a time station unless the motel is located after the time station; finally, consider an RV instead of a motel for more flexibility, if a good bed and shower are available in the RV.

12. THE 2016 RACE – A CHRONOLOGY

Now that the Honey Badger's winning race strategy has been laid out supported by race data, and preparation and execution have been reviewed in detail, it is a good idea for the reader to absorb the flow of the actual race narrative.

Dex Tooke, an experienced veteran racer and crew member of RAAM, has written a beautiful book on the race experience. Likewise, Amy Snyder's *Hell on Two Wheels* provides an account of the Open contenders (less so the Masters) with many informative details. This chapter is not meant to emulate those books, which the present authors strongly recommend to any racer for inspiration and information. Instead, we provide a brief but complete account of a winning race with actual situations as they occurred, in the context of our two major principles: regular rest, and riding at night. You will see the five keystones from Chapter 2 implemented almost without fail, day after day:

1. The racer sleeps about four hours per day.
2. The racer jet-lags to sleep in the middle of the day, when it is hottest.
3. Race uninterrupted for 19-21 hours through the night until late morning.
4. Make use of stationary crew exchanges for racer hygiene breaks.
5. Two crew members in three vehicles keeps crews busy yet rested.

The chronology of this chapter is to be contrasted with the clinically perfect description of the ideal situation in the rest of the book: The "reality versus the plan," so to speak. This chapter may be particularly useful for crews because our crew arrangement (only 2 crew in 3 follow vehicles, no shuttle vehicle) is somewhat unorthodox. Crews will see how the various duties were carried out in practice.

This chapter is organized as follows: RAAM 2016 is described shift by shift - first from the racer's perspective, then from the perspective of the three crews, which had different functions (Chapter 6). The evening crew (Crew #1) woke up the racer and guided him in the afternoon and past sunset, often by leapfrog. The night crew (Crew #2) took over during the night into the early morning hours, strictly in follow mode. And the morning crew (Crew #3) took care of the racer until the next sleep period in the late morning or early afternoon. Their key decision each day was how far the racer would go to get sufficient sleep to be able to ride consistently for 10 or more days.

The race personnel:

Racer: Martin Gruebele, "The Honey Badger," age 52

Crew #1 (evening): Julie Turner and her niece Lana Pohlmann
Nearly a year after agreeing to follow Martin on his quest to finish the Race Across America, Lana, who lives in Florida, flew to Illinois to stay at Julie's house. Julie is an avid cyclist, and Lana is an avid traveler, so they were confident that they would complement each other well as crew partners.

Crew #2 (night): Harry Zink and Roy Tylinski, joined by Jay Yost on Day 8
Harry wrangles computers and networks for a living, Roy was a barista (useful skill for late night shifts), and Jay directs Owens Funeral home (a skill we hoped not to utilize). Harry and Jay knew each other well from RAAM 2013, Roy and Jay knew each other in Champaign, and Roy and Harry bonded after many hours cooped up together during the practice race in March 2016.

Crew #3 (morning): Greg Scott and his father Dr. Ed Scott
University Professor and numbers-analyzer Greg and his father Ed, an off-duty physician, undertook the adventure as a father-son road adventure trip. Their comments show how important the daily rest is: while crew #1 always found the Honey Badger happy-go-lucky, crew #3 dealt with nodding off on the bike, slow riding, fidgeting off the bike, and other signs of fatigue.

PRE-RACE

The Illinois crew (Julie Turner, Roy Tylinski, Lana Pohlmann and Martin Gruebele, our racer) left Champaign on Thursday June 9th. Three follow vehicles were loaded with 4 bikes, 2 black milk crates for food/clothes supply that stayed with each van, and an additional 2 red special supplies crates to be swapped at crew exchanges. (Chapter 7 describes all supplies in detail.)

The evening crew (Julie, Lana) drove to Amarillo on the first day. The racer and night crew (Roy, Martin) drove further to Tucumcari: they were jet-lagging themselves to stay up all night during the race, in keeping with **keystone 2** of our race strategy. On the second day, the Illinois crew reached Oceanside, after a stop at the Grand Canyon for some sightseeing.

In Oceanside, we met up with Greg and Ed Scott, and Harry Zink, Martin's crew chief. Harry had already crewed The Honey Badger at RAAM two-man team in 2013, when Martin raced the course with Jay Yost for a 3rd place finish. There was some time to explore the beautiful resort town of Oceanside with its white sand beach, using our large rented house on Michigan Avenue as the base. A rented house is a much better base than a bunch of hotel rooms.

The weekend was busy (**keystone 5**). The crew prepped the three vehicles: a tan Caravan driven by the "Golden Girls" Julie and Lana, a white Expedition driven by the "Wyld Stallyns" Harry and Roy, and a black Expedition, the "Black Beast," driven by Greg and Ed. The cars needed amber rear flash lights, slow vehicle triangles, and race numbers that Martin had picked up from the race office at the Oceanside Beach along with the racer package. The non-magnetic Expeditions made for a mini-emergency, requiring a hitch attachment to mount the rear triangle. The Golden Girls got the two red equipment and special clothes crates in their van, since they would drive the first race shift.

On Sunday, the crew practiced crew exchanges. Martin rode a part of the course near Old Castle Road, where Crew #1 would begin leapfrog support after Martin rode the first 23 miles of RAAM alone. Here's what Julie said: "The most helpful thing for us was the practice crew exchanges and bottle hand-offs we did along the actual race route to get accustomed to the procedures. The majority of us had attended the practice race in March, where Martin rode a stretch of the official race route from Illinois to Ohio, where we got familiarized with the crew jobs, yet Old Castle Road was a good opportunity to get the whole team engaged leading up to the start."

On Sunday afternoon, we also attended the official crew meeting down by the pier, where we learned about what to expect while on the road, how to navigate with the route book, and most importantly, how to avoid penalties.

The Golden Girls put on bicycle wheel-themed nails for the occasion (left), and signed their crew van (right)

Crew members began to fall into their different roles: Roy the bike wrangler and repair specialist; Greg the numbers expert and planner; Julie providing food and keeping things well-organized; Lana the master-navigator; Ed providing reassurance about aches and pains; and Harry as the tech expert keeping an eye on Martin's sleep and schedule to make sure the racer would not cut corners. During the race, the crew chief (and not the racer) has the ultimate decision authority.

On Monday, Harry got Martin's iPhone power connector fixed, critical for keeping the racer's GPS information flowing during the race. We successfully passed the official inspection, and were all set to go. We attended the final racer briefing, where alerts about road conditions and route changes were announced. All the racers were introduced with big fanfare at the RAAM racer meeting on Monday evening. It was really interesting to hear the racers' stories and see participants from many different places in the world, ranging from the Americas to Europe and all the way from Asia.

The crew in reflective vests and ankle bands passing the inspection at the parking lot near RAAM Headquarters. The Caravan van holds a magnetic rear triangle.

Then it was the quiet before the storm, with a dinner of salmon and rice, and Martin bedding down late (5 AM Champaign time) so he could get up late and become accustomed to the night riding cycle (**keystone 2**).

Prior to the race, the strategy was worked out in detail (**keystones 1-5**): Martin would ride roughly 20 hours each day at *ca.* 100-110 bpm effort (except Day 1), interrupted by 10-15 minutes at crew exchanges, so the crews would have 6- to 7-hour shifts. Then Martin would bed down mid-day for about 4 hours, and repeat the cycle. The idea was to break the hot day riding (up to 100 °F in the desert in 2016) into a morning and an afternoon segment, and skip the 4 to 5 hottest hours of mid-day altogether. This is an unusual strategy not adopted by other Masters teams, who were following more conventional shorter breaks and more day riding.

Each crew had a well-defined task: Crew #1 was the afternoon crew: Julie and Lana would drive to Martin's motel, get everything prepped, wake him up for a quick breakfast, double check the RAAM GPS unit and all else was in place for the day's racing, and crew him for about 100 miles. Then Crew #2 would take over for the deep night shift, usually from around 23:00 to around 05:00. Harry and Roy had to be in follow mode all night, 30 feet behind Martin, so a full tank of gas, large bladders, and good spirits were the rules of the night. Finally, Crew #3 with Greg and Ed would take over. At 9 AM they could switch to "leapfrog mode," where the van can jump ahead and wait for the racer, rather than following straight behind. It was Crew #3's responsibility to get Martin to bed early enough for sleep, but not so early that we would fall behind schedule. With favorable west winds in the plains, about 10 days was the target, while we expected the Open male racers would take about 8.5 to 9 days. The overall winner would eventually take about 9.5 days, and the fastest Master, 11 days. Having a two-day buffer in your race plan against contingencies does deliver a certain feeling of security.

RACE DAY 1: June 14/15

Martin resting and hydrating in the air-conditioned meeting hall next to the start line, waiting for the RAW racers to get going before the solo RAAM start at 13:00

The racer: On Tuesday at 13:00, the solo racers were sent off, and Martin started the first 23 miles of the race alone. Crew #3 (Greg and Ed) paraded him out of the start line. Martin rode the Dimond Superbike on the relatively flat course to Old Castle Road where the Golden Girls were waiting. Martin's RideWithGPS performed flawlessly, and with few exceptions continued to do so for the remaining 3000 miles, guiding him at every turn so the crew did not have to give directions. When Crew #1 took over, Martin switched to the Merlin because climbs over the coastal range were coming up before the famed "Glass Elevator," a steep descent into Borrego Springs. There the temperature jumped to about 100 °F, but with a tailwind. Martin hopped back onto the Superbike, and time trialed his way through the night before the first stationary crew exchange near Brawley, and the second stationary crew exchange after Blythe (**keystone 4**). Greg and Ed put him to bed after 342 miles and 19h20m of riding to Salome, AZ (TS 5) at Sheffler's motel (**keystone 3**).

The Honey Badger off to the start, followed by Crew #3 in the "Black Beast."

The three crews: After feeding Martin a late granola breakfast (**keystone 2**), Julie and Lana arrived at the Oceanside Pier around noon, an hour before the solo racers would depart. Martin had found a comfortable bench inside of the Oceanside Visitor's Center. Crew #1 kept Martin company and hydrated him, so that he wouldn't nod off and miss his start time. Crew #3 waited in their follow vehicle for their cue from race staff to get rolling behind their racer.

As soon as Martin crossed the start line, the Golden Girls headed to the Trading Post parking lot on Old Castle Road. While waiting for Martin, Julie and Lana had the first real encounter with other racers' crews. An Italian team was fascinated by our magnetic slow moving triangle. Martin had fitted the triangle with magnets, secured by screws and wing nuts. At first glance, it looks as if the triangle is screwed into the back of the car. Julie easily popped it on and off the back of the car, and the Italians were very impressed. They jokingly tried to take it from our crew and put it on their vehicle. This is only one of many encounters we had with crew members from around the world. Then Martin came rolling up, and Crew #1 was on for their first leap frog support.

During the first 7-hour shift, about 115 miles into Arizona, Julie was initially concerned by so many crews on the same road, but it turned out to be a good thing. It was easy to spot where the good pull-off areas were, and everyone was excited and supportive of every racer and crew. Martin was staying well fueled and hydrated. After handing Martin off to Harry and Roy, Crew #1 drove about 140 miles to their hotel in Parker, AZ and got a good night's rest to be ready for the next day.

The busy parking lot at the Trading Post on Old Castle Road, where crews pick up their racer for the first time.

In the meantime, Crew #2 had watched Martin ride slowly down the start chute, on his mission to deliberately manage his energy from the beginning. During crew exchange, the crews traded some amazing local strawberries for local dates. The road was essentially straight for the night shift. Temperatures were cooler during the night (**keystone 3**), but the heat still required ice-cold bottles and salt tablets every hour throughout the night shift. The crew shuddered at the thought of what racers would encounter in the desert during the day. While dodging sand drifts, Martin's eye irritation started.

Crew #3 had driven the Black Beast behind the Honey Badger in the parade start, then headed to the Budget Host in Blythe to rest. On the way, they got a text from Harry: all support vehicles, including those not following, needed to have headlights on at all times. This was a constant challenge because the Ford Expedition turns off the daytime headlights when you get out of the vehicle. It was 100 °F outside, but the clerk at the motel said it that it was cool for this time of year. Greg and Ed ran errands to get gas, ice, and a Subway sandwich for Martin (**keystone 5**).

Ed driving at sunrise on the first day of the race.

Crew #3 went to bed late at 21:30, and Harry woke them up early around 00:45 PDT, several hours ahead of schedule. After prepping in the parking lot, the second exchange of the day happened smoothly around 01:30. Martin rode well and was hours ahead of schedule. After Parker, we turned onto a road with a stiff headwind and a rough surface and Martin's cadence dropped considerably on the way to Salome. Martin ate only sports nutrition (gels, bars, HEED/Gatorade mix) and some pretzels for salt. He said his stomach didn't feel well enough to eat a sandwich on the bike, and he ate it at the motel instead. A full meal a day was an important side effect of the regular motel stays. The room that Greg had originally reserved in Salome was not available. Crew #2 (Roy and Harry) vacated their room for Martin, while another room was readied by the hotel maids. While Martin slept, crews #2 and #3 grabbed breakfast across the street, and made plans for the next day. Then Crew #3 drove to the Happy Jack Lodge between Camp Verde and Flagstaff, stopping for groceries and supplies in Camp Verde.

RACE DAY 2: June 15/16

The racer: After getting up in the afternoon (**keystone 2**), Martin hopped on the superbike, eventually switching to the Merlin because of serious climbing between Yarnell Pass and Flagstaff (TS 9). Throughout the night, Crew #2 kept him well fed with beef jerky (salt and protein[18]), gels (2+ portions), energy bars (2+), drink (a bottle of 50% HEED, 50% Gatorade per hour), and a chicken sandwich. This was to be the main food routine throughout the race. We did not deviate from it significantly except before rest breaks, when Martin had time to digest heavier food, such as pizza.

The monotony of night riding was interrupted by Paul Ponder, a stand-by crew member, who had come to Jerome, AZ and shot some photos of Martin on the course (photo next page). Soon thereafter, it was time to switch to the morning crew. Greg and Ed prepped the bike, changed crates with Harry and Roy, and got everything ready for the next shift, while Martin took 10 minutes to perform his hygiene routine. Every sensitive spot was cleaned with iodine solution, antibiotic cream, and layered with benzocaine cream and Vaseline to avoid saddle sores, infections, and minimize pain. He did this 4 times a day – at every crew exchange and at bedtime (**keystone 4**), which proved successful: while Martin gradually got chafed after 3000 miles, never a sore or infection developed. The day's ride to Flagstaff (TS 9) was only 252 miles due to heavy climbing.

The Honey Badger climbing Yarnell Pass

The three crews: Lana looked forward to seeing the large cacti in the Arizona desert, and indeed Crew #1 spotted quite a few on the way to Martin's motel. Julie and Lana arrived at the motel in plenty of time to organize supplies for the next shift. Roy updated Crew #1 on Martin's well-being.

This was Martin's first sleep break, and he awoke easily at 14:00 when Crew #1 entered his motel room. Apparently 4 hours of sleep was just right for our racer to awake naturally (**keystone 1**). The daily "morning" task was to feed our racer a cereal breakfast, make sure all of his gear was lined up and ready, and all crates and his hygiene backpack were stowed in the crew van before leaving the hotel room. While Martin got back onto his bike, Lana called the RAAM headquarters, announcing he was ready to go back on course. Martin would have a set of questions while he was getting ready, for which we needed to know the answers (**keystone 5**). He wanted to know the daily weather forecast, upcoming elevation changes, and the distance to the next time stations.

The Honey Badger and the "Wyld Stallyns" (crew #2) descending through Jerome (photo by Paul Ponder).

The days were busy and exhausting for the crew. Julie and Lana quickly got into the habit of handing Martin his drink bottle partly filled, instead of him keeping the bottle on the bike for long. This worked for two reasons: his bottle would always be cold,[22] and we could ensure he would drink every 15 minutes, so he could not forget. He had a lot of climbing to do in the West, and dealt with temperature extremes (90 to 100 °F in the day, 40s at night). At times the crew battled with fatigue in the late evening hours, but Martin was still going strong.

Julie and Lana quickly learned about the dangers of running car engines while parked on dry desert grass. Luckily, they did not set the desert on fire but it was a close call! Lana also learned (the hard way) the importance of looking down before leaping out of the passenger side, just in case Julie had parked on an incline, and there was a slippery sand hill leading to a ditch full of cacti.

The Golden Girls and some serious cacti on the route

Crew #2 got some more sleep in their second room at the Salome motel, after Martin pre-empted their first room. The crew exchange on the eastern side of Prescott went well, but there was an issue with the Giant TCR0 dropping out of the large ring. Roy kept busy with mechanical adjustments and feeding Martin at the same time (**keystone 5**). After a steady push, Martin layered up clothes and zipped down through Jerome. Soon, the route started going up again and Crew #2 ferried Martin past several miles of fresh oil on the road, as per instructions from RAAM headquarters. As he climbed out of Camp Verde, Martin trudged on, but temperatures dropped very close to freezing and pushed the limits of his clothing. The racer then encountered another eye irritant: wildfire smoke. This must have added to Martin's red-eye problems, which had gotten worse on Day 2.

Crew #3 met Harry and Roy at a pullout just north of the lodge. When Martin rolled up, he said "I need you to set the car to 80° and I need one person from each crew in the vehicle to discuss, while the other two take care of the bikes." It was below 45 °F and Martin was cold, particularly his hands. The crew cranked the heat up some more, and Harry and Greg climbed into the vehicle with the Honey Badger while he changed and warmed up. At 41 minutes, this was one of our slowest crew exchanges. The goal had been to make it to Cameron, but based on the time it was decided that Martin would stop 50 miles short in Flagstaff (**keystone 2**).

Greg and Martin talking about the day's plan during the crew exchange, while Martin warms up after a cold ride past the Camp Verde time station.

Martin's entire morning ride was tough and slow-going after the cold. During the 55 miles, he had one energy bar and two gel portions, but no sandwich. As the morning warmed up, Martin slowly shed layers. One of his booties was lost during one of the layer-shedding stops. When Martin reached a few miles of one-lane road closure (logging to reduce the spread of a wildfire), a flagger tried to send Martin on through alone, but the crew was in direct-follow. Martin waited, and then rode through with his crew's vehicle and the pilot car. The pilot car drove ahead, and as Martin continued riding, the pilot car came back at him with traffic from the other direction! Martin and his crew vehicle had to pull off quickly and scramble out of the way.

Meanwhile Crew #2 had driven to Flagstaff and gotten themselves and Martin rooms at a Motel 6. Greg and Ed went with Martin past the Motel 6 to the time station, called in the time station, put Martin in the car, and drove back to the Motel 6 to put him to sleep after feeding him. Julie and Lana showed up shortly thereafter, so all three crew vehicles were together in the parking lot. While the night crew slept, four of the crew went out for lunch, and to REI to buy replacement booties (on sale!).

Martin getting back on the bike after the June 16 crew exchange before Flagstaff, AZ.

Crew #3 then drove ahead to Mexican Hat, UT, through the Navajo and Hopi reservations and Monument Valley. They booked rooms for themselves and Crew #1 stayed at the Canyonlands Motel, where the sinks and tubs were pink. Greg and Ed drove a few miles to see The Goosenecks (**keystone 5**), went for a short run and spent some time explaining to a French couple that the race did not take place in "easy stages" like *Le Tour de France*. Ed talked to an Australian on a motorcycle who had done a lot of bicycling in Australia. Then Crew #3 bought food, gas, and ice at the gas station, and shared a burger at the "Swinging Steak."

RACE DAY 3: June 16/17

The racer: Martin was a little worried: he had lost feeling in one of his left toes, and his eyes were bloodshot and swollen. From here on, Martin almost exclusively wore the shoes he had used for RAAM 2013, as he suspected the new shoes had too small a toe box, although they had felt fine over 1000s of miles of training. Ed had a look at Martin's eyes, and got some eye drops at a local pharmacy. The redness was most likely due to dry air and sand blowing in the desert. On the way to Durango, a Canadian racer rode into the split between two cow grates and DNFd. At the same time, miles ahead, Martin reached a three-mile gravel section. RAAM management had decided that tired riders could get through this on their road bikes. Martin fishtailed on a 6% descent followed by a deep gravel curve, but somehow managed to stay upright. Male Open racer Aske Søby was not so lucky: he had crashed a few hours earlier on the same spot and was hospitalized. After Mexican Hat (TS 12 in Utah), Martin was unable to get his heart rate above 110 bpm, and it would stay that way for most of the race: the fatigue of 19 hours/day riding and 4 hours of sleep took its toll, and reduced his maximum output power as expected (**keystones 1 to 3**). Nonetheless, Martin was moving up the ranks with steady riding.

The three crews: Martin had assured the crews that, by Day 3, they would get into the swing of things. This was most definitely the case. Getting Martin up and ready to go was much easier for Crew #1. The most effective procedures became second nature. They perfected their bottle hand-offs just before it was time for mandatory follow mode on the Navajo Indian reservation, ranging from Arizona into Utah. The scenery was beautiful, and Julie and Lana often caught Martin taking a glimpse away from the road, staring into the desert sunset or mesas. After leaving Martin with Crew #2 in good spirits, Julie and Lana made their way through Monument Valley, the views hidden at night. With a few hours to spare in the morning (**keystone 5**), Crew #1 got another close look at some of the rock monuments in the area, especially the infamous "Mexican Hat" formation. Julie and Lana concluded that Monument Valley was definitely worth a future visit.

The Wyld Stallyns. Each crew got a nickname, and Roy and Harry settled on this sticker for their white Expedition SUV, although they usually did a Blues Brothers routine in the car.

In the meantime, Roy on Crew #2 had diagnosed the TCRO problem: the housing to the shifter was a little short, and it had been popping out of the cable guide when the front wheel was turned 90 degrees to put the bike in the crew vans. Re-routing the cable housing fixed this problem. Halfway through the Navajo Reservation, Crew #2 picked up Martin. Temperatures dropped, and Harry put a jacket on Martin. When rolling out, Martin's earbud got tangled up in the spokes. Luckily, there was no crash, and quick work with Roy's utility knife got Martin moving again. Fewer salt tablets were required while riding through Utah this night. A quick crew exchange followed after a few steady climbs before entering Colorado.

It became standard protocol during the race for crews to send each other photos by text message of where they were staged to make finding the crew exchanges easier. Crew #3 sent this photo to Crew #2 from Bluff, UT for the exchange. It is one of the many ideas the crews came up with during the race to improve efficiency.

Crew #3 got its wake-up call from Harry and drove ahead of the active Crew #2 to Bluff, UT to set up for the exchange. A crew member from another rider walked up. He said that their crew had 10 people and they were using three vehicles. Two vehicles were in active support (one following with three people, one leapfrogging with two people) and the third vehicle was shuttling the other 5 people forward. This meant that, despite having a larger crew than the Honey Badger, they were working longer shifts (**keystone 5**).

After the exchange, Crew #3 and the racer entered western Colorado and passed one of the RAAM Masters leaders. Near the end of a gravel section, a police officer stopped Crew #3 to ask if they had passed a racer in a serious accident. When Greg told him "no," he sped off, followed a few minutes later by an ambulance. The crew later learned that a racer had crashed on a cattle grate a few miles back.

Crew #3 entered leapfrog mode just after the gravel section. Martin's phone backup battery died, and the spare was missing from the red crate. Greg gave the Honey Badger his phone, so he would have RideWithGPS for the rest of the day. Greg fed our racer a Wal-som to help him sleep when he stopped 15 miles later in Durango. Martin got to bed a couple of hours behind the 10-day schedule, but early enough for him to fall asleep easily (**keystone 2**).

Reaching the summit at Wolf Creek Pass. It was cold, but the Honey Badger wasn't, thanks to his clothing layers tested at Paris-Brest-Paris in 2015.

All crews had arrived in Durango, and took the TCR0 (which had developed more shifter trouble) to the Velomotion bike shop. It turned out that there was nothing wrong with the shifter mechanism except for old age, and the tech quickly tuned it up free of charge. It's great to have cycling Samaritans along the road. Shopping for gloves and running many other errands kept all crew members busy during Martin's entire sleep (**keystone 5**).

Crew #3 had a hard time finding a place to stay in eastern Colorado because there was a motorcycle event in Alamosa. They finally found a place to stay at the Fort Garland Motor Inn. The owner was very proud of her motel, and was concerned Ed was going to make a mess washing Martin's laundry in the sink. Ed convinced her otherwise, and she even gave him some clothes hangers to help get everything dried.

RACE DAY 4: June 17/18

The racer: Martin started in Durango with Crew #1 rather late, and this delay from schedule would have a bad effect at the end of the shift. After some serious climbing, the Golden Girls cheered Martin over Wolf Creek Pass, and a warm jacket that Roy had supplied saved Martin on the ice cold descent. At the top, he bantered with some RAW and RAAM crews. This happened often during the race: cheers for the Honey Badger from other crews, and our crew cheering on other racers. It really felt like quite the family affair. After a quiet shift with Harry and Roy through Alamosa, cruising along as planned, Greg and Ed escorted Martin to the final destination of the day: out of the Rockies, to Trinidad (TS 20) in eastern Colorado. The descent to La Veta (TS 19) from the 9418 ft. La Veta summit was the most beautiful thing Martin had ever seen in the US: the valley is like a magical area, with rock pillars, forested glades, small villages, azure lakes, blue mountains in the distance, like a Disneyland of all the beautiful sights in the US shepherded into a single valley.

Martin descending to La Veta, one of the most beautiful sights of RAAM.

Martin was a few hours behind schedule, and La Veta would have been the ideal rest stop. Instead, it was decided to forge on to TS 20, and this was the largest departure from Martin's planned rest schedule during RAAM (**keystone 2** was violated here). Martin was tired and very slow on the climb to Cuchara summit, and on the rollers with a headwind that led out of the mountains. Martin reached Trinidad exhausted and too far beyond his sleep schedule: He has a strong circadian clock, and once the 24-hour mark is passed, he stays awake.

The three crews: Crew #1 started late with Martin, which was nice because there was much less traffic up to the summit and on the descent from Wolf Creek Pass. Julie and Lana were excited to accompany Martin on this special passage of the race across the Continental Divide. This was also where they learned that the red special clothing crate had its uses, as Martin started putting on layer after layer as he climbed and finally flew down the breezy descent at near-freezing temperatures.

After waiting for 3 hours, Crew #2 started their shift. The day went smoothly as Martin raced non-stop through temperatures well below 40 (**keystone 3**). Shortly after passing the Rio Grande, the sun rose over Mt. Blanca (14,351 ft.). Roy was feeding Martin all the food he had available, and it was obvious that the climbs had taken their caloric toll. Racer fatigue and tunnel vision seemed to be in play as Martin almost rode past Greg from Crew #3, who was dancing around in all his reflective gear at the crew exchange.

Night Crew #2 getting some R & R at the pool before heading to sleep in Trinidad, CO

After receiving the usual early morning wakeup call and quietly exiting the motel, Crew #3 accompanied Martin over the eastward ranges of the Rockies. After La Veta, Crew #3 stopped for a handoff at a pullout with views of Profile Rock and Devil's Staircase. As advertised in the route book, Cuchara Pass is one of the most scenic in Colorado, but SR12, The Highway of the Legends, is narrow and curvy. Ed had to use 4-wheel drive to extract the vehicle from one of the few pullouts available. On this stretch, the media van came along and did an extensive interview and photo shoot as Martin continued his relentless climb up the 6% grade to the summit at 9939 feet. Martin then passed Monument Lake and North Lake. As he passed the handoff area opposite one of these lakes he turned, smiled and said "It's like a painting." Unfortunately, the hoped-for smooth descent with a tailwind into Trinidad did not materialize, and a tired Martin took much longer than anticipated to cover the remaining 37 miles, while the temperature rose at the lower elevation. Finally, Martin arrived at time station 20 at the historic City Hall. After Martin consumed a much-anticipated pizza (delivered by Harry and Roy), he was settled into bed.

Martin getting a sandwich during a leap-frog exchange on the climb to La Cuchara Pass.

After days of eye drops, Martin's eyes were looking better, but Martin had gotten to bed too late. All crews gathered to discuss a shorter ride the next day, to get back on the mid-day sleep schedule to avoid the heat (**keystone 2**). Crew #3 then drove ahead to Springfield, CO, to the Stage Stop Hotel. Martin's meals for the next day were purchased, and Greg arranged for Crew #2 to stay in the room after Crew #3, to cut down on costs.

RACE DAY 5: June 18/19

The racer: After lying in bed half-awake for almost 4 hours, Martin tackled the eastern Colorado and Kansas plains. Instead of the hoped-for 10 mph SW seasonal tailwind across the Midwest, Martin's (and the other racers') worst fear came true: a SE headwind was blowing up to 15 mph. Fortunately, Martin had a secret weapon. The Dimond Superbike cuts through headwinds better than any other time trial bike, and made the middle 800 miles of RAAM tolerable. Harry wisely decided to make it a shorter day. Martin rode only 195 miles to get back on the planned mid-day sleeping schedule, and to split the hot part of the day in two (**keystone 2**). The shorter day would also bring the crews back on schedule. And none too soon: near Johnson City, KS, Martin fell asleep on the bike and rode off into the grasslands on the right side of the road. Fortunately, he veered right instead of left when going slack. Greg and Ed got a little worried, and started chatting with Martin to make sure he would make it to Ulysses (TS 23) awake. Going to bed, Martin felt generally horrible after missing his sleep the day before, but more determined than ever to ramp it up again the next day. The Honey Badger don't care! The whole episode could have been avoided by resting in La Veta, or by having an RV available for the racer instead of delaying the motel stop. Still, the long ride to Trinidad was the only significant deviation from an otherwise seamlessly executed race plan (**keystone 2**).

Julie and Lana celebrate "Goodbye Colorado and Hello, Kansas!"

The three crews: Julie and Lana enjoyed the drive to Martin's hotel in the remaining beautiful mountain ranges of Colorado. When Crew #1 went to wake Martin, they found him awake: he hadn't slept well because of the delayed rest break. Despite his lack of sleep, he started the first crew shift with his usual optimism. Direct follow mode, required at the late start time of the shift, works out better when you have a tired racer. Lana constantly watched, fed and hydrated Martin, as Julie rolled up easily next to him to make sure he was okay. Martin gave the crew his happy thumbs up at regular intervals. As he entered the Kansas plains, Martin encountered a strong headwind. This took a lot of energy to ride against, and Crew #2 was advised that Martin was very tired. Crew chief Harry made it a short day for Martin to bring the whole rest period back to a mid-day schedule.

Meanwhile, Crew #2 put in a little shut-eye in Trinidad. Roy got up early to do the regular chores of gas and food. Harry had to deal with a client, so Crew #2 was a little delayed and caught up with the racer just after midnight. At the crew exchange, stiff cross- and headwinds were making it hard to run around the cars. Roy was unable to switch rims to a set with shallower, wind-friendly profiles due to a width difference, so Martin rode the tri-spokes into the howling winds. He was in good spirits, but signaling a little less than usual because his line was more than a bit wobbly in the strong cross winds. Not much happened throughout the night, as Martin rhythmically powered through the moonlit plains of eastern Colorado and Kansas without a stop (**keystone 3**).

Kansas sunrise

Crew #3 staged on the outskirts of Springfield, ready for a short (~200 miles) day to Ulysses, KS. The stiff crosswind coming from the southeast continued to make riding tough. Shortly after crossing into Kansas, Martin stopped pedaling momentarily and veered toward the right edge of the road. Crew #3 immediately realized that he had fallen asleep on the bike. Martin jerked to an awakened state as he went off the road. Fortunately, the drop from the shoulder to the grass was small, and Martin did not over-react. He rode into the grass and coasted to a stop. Greg jumped out of the car to talk with Martin and he admitted that he had dozed off. For the rest of the ride into Ulysses, Greg set a timer and pulled up frequently to make sure our racer was not getting too drowsy. Some notable conversations between Greg and Martin during this stretch:

- "Martin, you weren't listening to Ravel when you fell asleep, were you?" "No, Schubert." "Don't you have any Beastie Boys on there?" (rolls his eyes) "No."
- "Martin, why did I get an email from you in Durango when you were sleeping, asking me to referee a paper for a science journal?" "The work never stops."
- "Martin, do you want a riddle?" "No. No mind games."

- Martin waved us up just to tell us, "The fog lines were painted in a linear fashion. You can't tell just by looking at a painted fog line, but when you look at it relative to a bicycle wheel at speed, you can see the streaks in the paint."
- About 15 miles outside of Ulysses, Martin said "I know you're not going to like this, but I'm going to need the Wal-som now so that I can actually fall asleep when we get to the motel."

When Crew #3 reached the Ulysses city limit sign, Martin threw his fist into the air in a victory salute. He was clearly happy to be done and ready for some rest. Ed put him to bed at the Corporate Hotel East just past TS 23. Crew #1 was sleeping there, and when they got up, the two crews talked and then texted Crew #2. The crew voted unanimously to give Martin an extra hour of sleep, even if he wouldn't be happy about it when he woke up. Everyone was confident that the Honey Badger would sleep well after his restless night the day before, and that is indeed what happened.

Crew #3 drove ahead to Kingman, KS and stayed at the Copa Motel. The place looked very run-down on the outside, but had surprisingly new and remodeled rooms. Greg and Ed went out for a run on a dirt road, conveniently located directly behind the motel. The road was the site for a local 50k race, which would be a pretty boring 50k, but was a nice place to run for a few miles. After their run, Greg and Ed used the pool to cool off and then hung their clothes and Martin's clothes out to dry. Greg ran the gas and food errands and picked up some Chinese take-out for a Father's Day meal with Ed by the pool (**keystone 5**).

RACE DAY 6: June 19/20

The racer: The Golden Girls awakened Martin after a solid 4.5-hour sleep, ordered by Harry to make up for the previous sleepless night. It worked like a charm. Martin's eye was less red, his foot less bothersome, and he felt strong again. The crews had settled into their routines and were working like well-honed clockwork, as were Martin's legs. That day, Martin put in 328 miles across the Kansas plains, mostly in a light headwind. The superbike did the job it was paid to do, enabling an average on-bike speed of 18 mph in the headwind, despite Martin's legs being tired from riding 1800 miles so far. The nutrition program outlined earlier continued. Martin was eating better now, devouring more sandwich and extra gel to make up for a large part of the energy deficit of *ca.* 7200 kcal/day. That night, for the first time during the race, Martin tasted the wonders of caffeine. As he was approaching Maize (TS 27) with Harry and Roy, his heart rate had dropped from 110 bpm earlier in the day to an abysmal 75 bpm and he was riding 13 mph. Not having had much caffeine in weeks, the Honey Badger took a 300 mg caffeine pill from his emergency supply Ziploc bag, and swallowed it with a gel. 15 minutes later, a miracle began: Martin sped up steadily from 13 to 20 mph as his heart rate went from 75 back to 110. He rode fast the rest of the night and the next day. Greg threw in another 100 mg six hours after the first dose, based on his dosage calculations (Figure 8.3). Caffeine dramatically reduces the perceived effort sensed by the brain's central governor, which limits the rate of exertion to ensure glucose reserves for the brain.[23] Martin now felt that the 110 bpm pedaling was comparable to 75 bpm pedaling before the caffeine. The crew kept up this caffeination schedule for the rest of the race, and although its effect diminished day after day, it still worked a little even at the end.

Martin's strategy of sleeping during the hot mid-day hours and splitting the day in half was starting to pay off. Everyone else had been taking shorter and more irregular naps throughout the day and night, which Martin had previously concluded would do him no good, as he needed two REM cycles of at least 1-½ hours each, plus a half hour to nod off, to be adequately rested (**keystone 1**). With the exception of Day 5, Martin usually slept almost 4 hours, which proved to have him well-rested for the next ride. As The Honey Badger approached Missouri, the other racers were beginning to struggle more, and started to fall behind Martin except during sleep breaks.

On the plains of Kansas

The three crews: The last couple of shifts had been long and late for Crew #1, due to Martin riding longer in the morning hours and sleeping later into the afternoon. Now they were back on schedule and everything was running smoothly again. The crews were regularly communicating, sharing challenges and funny stories along the way.

Roy helping Martin dismount the Superbike during a stationary exchange from Crew #1 to Crew #2 (crew chief Harry on the right)

Crew #2 drove on from the prior night's crew exchange in Springfield to Ulysses, KS. Harry got his first taste of Sonic food ... there probably won't be a repeat. Roy chatted with lovely local volunteers at a manned time station. They asked Roy to reveal the mystery behind the Honey Badger's name, which was a fair trade for homemade pumpkin cranberry muffins. Further on at Greensburg KS, Crew #2 picked up Martin for an exciting shift. Three quarters of the way to Pratt, the next time station, the Wyld Stallyns pulled up next to Martin, blaring *"Livin' on a Prayer,"* as they passed the 1545-mile halfway point. So began the counting of the miles backwards. Martin was keen to point out the first Casey's General Store and his sudden desire for apple fritters. While passing through Kingman, Martin finally had his first flat, caused by a stray bead wire in the road. A quick switch of bikes and Roy's expertise as back seat mechanic while Harry was driving, and the problem was no more. With Martin buzzing on a caffeine tablet all night (**keystone 3**), Crew #2 made it just past TS 27, Maize, KS to hand off to Crew #3. At this point in the race, Harry and Roy had become very tired because of the day sleeping and night driving, to which neither had acclimatized as fully as the racer. They called up Crew #3 a bit early to make the switch. Night crew fatigue was becoming a problem, but there was a solution: a backup crew member was available in Effingham to help out Crew #2.

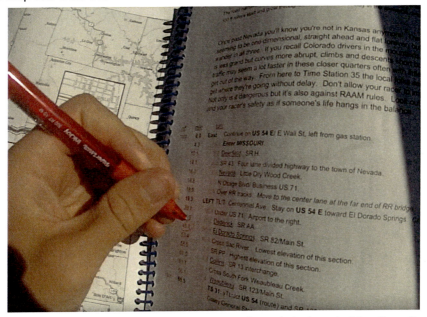

Roy making notes in the route book on the way to El Dorado Springs, deciding the optimal crew exchange point for shift 7.

After the early wake-up call from Crew #2, Crew #3 arranged to sleep a bit longer and jump ahead to Maize, KS to pick up Martin just west of Wichita. He was making good time and it was hard for Ed and Greg to catch up. They finally jumped past the Honey Badger just past the time station, and set up for the exchange at the Arkansas River. Martin was suddenly hungry for a lot of gel. Crew #2 realized we would run low on gel by the end of the trip, so they arranged for backup crew member Jay Yost to bring some when he met the crew in Effingham, IL.

Martin had a good day, and he did some leap-frogging with the Aske Søby team. Martin and Aske rode together for a few minutes, and the crews stopped to chat. One of Aske's crew members loved getting on the PA to shout about how the "Honey Badger didn't give a s&%t."

Ed got Martin settled at the Townsman Motel in Yates Center, KS. It was right next to a Casey's, and Martin asked Greg for a specific donut, an apple fritter.

When Greg returned with a cake donut (because there were no apple fritters available), Martin said he didn't want it. Racers can have peculiarly specific urges on the road!

Crew #3 then drove ahead to Osage Beach, MO at the Lake of the Ozarks, and stayed at the Scottish Inn. They swam at the public beach before running errands. At a Dick's Sporting Goods they bought Martin some of the cheap Asics running socks that he likes cycling in, and then they ran food and gas errands. They arranged for a late checkout at the motel for a small fee, so that Harry and Roy could sleep in the room afterwards.

Chatting with a friendly Danish crew at a wide pull-out

RACE DAY 7: June 20/21

The racer: Martin was now regularly passing other Masters and Open racers, steadily moving up in the ranks and hovering around 1 to 3 instead of 6 to 7 among Masters. Past Fort Scott, he entered Missouri, which had serious climbs all over the place. Martin remembered the Ozarks around Camdenton from 2013, bit his tongue, turned up the music, and climbed hard. There were many nice fans and bystanders in Missouri, who made a much better impression on Martin than in 2013. For once in the race, in order to stay on the mid-day sleep schedule, the crew and Martin went a few miles off course to a motel in Owensville. A thunderstorm had caught up with him, and Martin had ridden it in the rain for hours. An RV for the racer's sleep break would have saved about a half hour.

The RAAM media crew interviewing the Honey Badger in Missouri.

The three crews: The Golden Girls entered Missouri around dusk. Martin had climbs and rain showers to deal with. Yet Lana and Julie could tell he was feeling good because they would get frequent thumbs up and "Hey, Golden Girls!" The Honey Badger told the Girls bits of trivia about his 2013 two-man RAAM race here and there. Crew #1 had the drink and food routines down to a science. They always had a nice crispy sandwich ready during their shift, compared to the soggy food served by the male crews. The simple secret? Stick the food in a Ziploc bag and then in the cooler, not directly on top of the wet ice bag. Crew #1 was in direct follow mode, so they kept the water bottles in the van. Every fifteen minutes Martin drank (RAAM allows four hand-offs per hour), and every hour he ate. Crew #1 worked best if Julie drove and Lana navigated. Never having spent more than a family weekend together, they got along really well, and had many jokes and stories to tell. Along the way, there were many Missouri fans cheering on the racers from the side of the road, and houses and towns were decorated with welcome signs. Of course the racer was also passed by countless cars and semi-trucks all across the country, and was quickly able to tell apart a "friendly" short honk from an "angered" long one.

While Crew #1 was inching forward, Crew #2 was held up by an urgent business call for Harry, and it was too late to get from El Dorado, KS, to El Dorado Springs, MO in time for the planned exchange. Fortunately, Martin didn't miss a beat on his shift, although he reminded Crew #2 that they owed the Golden Girls for crewing him some extra distance that day. The crews had one goal, and one crew helped out another when it was needed. Pedaling on with Crew #2, Martin kept a steady cadence over mostly flat terrain. The weather promised to bring some storms that were blowing to the southeast, on a collision course with the race route. Once RAAM's first rain hit, the crew ducked under an overpass near Camdenton to suit up Martin. As Nature (or Murphy's Law) would have it, the rain immediately lessened, so Martin straddled the line of being ready for harder rain, and sweating himself silly in the rain gear. Crew #2 rode that tightrope all the way past Lake Ozark where Martin was turned over to Crew #3.

Roy points at the live online tracking, showing the Honey Badger in 1st place among Masters for the first time during RAAM. The end of Day 7 was the first day the crew was allowed to tell Martin about the race standings.

Crew #3 got its wake-up call and exchanged between Osage Beach and Etterville, MO. Crew and racer were approaching Jefferson City at rush hour, and a major route change meant Martin's cues from RideWithGPS would not work. It was raining in fits and starts. The crew was in mandatory direct follow mode even though it was daylight and rush hour as they navigated through the city, and they had to use their emergency honk-signaling system frequently to keep Martin on course. It was stressful in the heavy traffic, but finally they made it through to US 50 for the long route detour. Martin rode through highly variable conditions on US 50. He got the attention of the RAAM media van for a long stretch. At one point, the plastic bag tied around his shoe to keep out rain was leaking, and Greg spilled water into the shoe while trying to fix the problem. The crew swapped Martin's socks and gave him a new plastic bag in the rain. "Misery in Missouri," as Ed put it. The crew decided to have Martin rest before the Washington time station, to avoid another late bedtime. Martin was called off-course where the crew drove him 11 miles to the Owensville Motor Inn. The owners only charged $30 since Martin was only using the room for a few hours – the best deal of the trip!

Greg had planned to change out some brake pads while Martin slept, but the tool kit was missing from the red tool crate. After some panic, he called Crew #2, who had forgotten to put the tools back in the crate after a flat tire fix. They had to drive ahead early to get the tools to Crew #1, so the active crew would not be without tools. Crew #3 re-inventoried all the crates, and determined that they would need more spare lithium batteries. This became a recurring theme of the race because the new RAAM rules required daytime lights on the bikes, and the lithium AA cells were expensive and hard to find. Crew #3 then drove ahead to Altamont, IL (near Effingham) to stay at the Altamont Motel. They walked downtown to get some dinner and took care of some other errands at a Casey's.

Crossing the Mississippi late on June 21st.

RACE DAY 8: June 21/22

The racer: After Lana and Julie drove a well-rested Martin back on the course from Owensville to route 50 near Rosebud, they zipped through Washington to the Mighty Mississippi, which was crossed at TS 35 at West Alton late on June 21. Now in Illinois, Martin felt better and better. His eyes were clearing up thanks to the high humidity, and his right foot had settled into a numb routine. He pressed on to Effingham (TS 37), where Jay Yost joined the crew in the early morning hours. Arizona was the last time Martin had enjoyed a nice tailwind, and he was now about 12 hours behind schedule, so it looked like an 11-day race. Every other racer had suffered the same winds, and the Open male racers were also half a day slower than in an "easy" year. Martin crossed from IL into IN in the early morning, passing through 3 states in 1 day. In Sullivan (TS 38), Martin's wife Nancy and daughter Valerie, his research group, and the physical chemistry support staff (Theresa, Beth, Karen) surprised him with some cheers, and he stopped for a photo op. A little later, our racer also got some cheers from Greg Youngen, who used to ride with Martin's cycling team, the "Wild Cards." Martin had instructed the crew not to update him about other racers until Day 8. One has to ride one's own race, commensurate with ability and sufficient rest, not beyond - so that the last 2 to 3 days can be parlayed into a win. When Martin was first informed of his standing in the race, and learned that he was at the front of the Masters' race, it was welcome and energizing news. Greg and Ed bedded Martin down on schedule at a motel in Linton for the mid-day rest period (**keystone 2**).

The Wild Card Cycling Team in Effingham just before sunrise. From left: Jay Yost, who joined Crew #2 at Effingham to help the tired night shift drivers, Neil Fortner, Jeff Turner, The Honey Badger, and Scott Dahman.

The three crews: As Crew #1 got closer to the mighty Mississippi River, driving got a bit tricky. There always seemed to be a line of cars behind the van, some more agitated than others. Julie checked the rearview mirror, and there was only one car, but then all the sudden there were five. Crew #1 tried their best to get Martin through the windy roads quickly without impeding traffic, but this was a feat. The crew had to give him a short-long honk signal several times, which meant he had to stop and let cars pass. As the crew crossed the Mississippi River, they could tell that Martin had a little more pep, just being back in Illinois. This, after all, was familiar territory for everyone. After completing the crew exchange in Alton, IL Crew #1 decided to make a longer drive to a hotel in Effingham, so Julie could see her husband Jeff at the Effingham time station. It meant a much shorter sleep schedule for Crew #1, but it was worth seeing Julie's husband and some of the Wild Card Cycling Team who had come to cheer Martin on.

Crew #2 headed across the Mississippi River ahead of the racer to be greeted by RAAM fans, and to set up the crew exchange. Illinois roads are a tunnel through a mountain of cornfields. Shortly into their shift, Roy and Harry celebrated with Martin for hitting the total distance of this year's Tour De France, advertised in the RAAM route book. Martin and Harry were shouting back and forth in French, with the crew putting on awful duct tape mustaches, "C'est magnifique!" The rest of the night, Martin ate and drank right on schedule every 15 minutes, and rode without a stop (**keystone 3**). The only interesting thing was a town called Funkhouser ... OK, Crew #2 was incredibly tired and desperate for diversions.

Martin leaves TS 37 (the High School in Effingham), followed by the "Black Beast." Follow mode was allowed east of the Mississippi even during the day, and the crew used it whenever the road was wide enough to allow following without hindering traffic.

Relief came at the end of Roy and Harry's shift in Effingham. There, a few Wild Card riders, including Jeff Turner (Julie's husband), Scott Dahman, Neil Fortner, and Jay Yost, waited for Crew #2 and the racer. As planned by Martin, Jay joined Crew #2, who had become the most tired from their midnight schedule and needed a fresh driver. Roy, Harry and their new driver Jay left Martin to finish his day with Crew #3.

Crew #3 staged for the exchange in Effingham on the left side of the road. Since the rules required all support to be done on the right side, they made sure to ask the RAAM staff volunteers whether it was okay to exchange on the left, to avoid a penalty. Martin chatted for a few minutes, and then got on the road with Ed and Greg. As they approached Indiana, Greg took a nice video of Martin's "Pavlovian response to the cowbell." They had trained him a few days before to drink when they rang the cowbell because it was not always possible to pull up next to him to remind him of his 15-minute, ¼-bottle drink routine, which he followed like a clockwork throughout the race. Greg texted with Martin's wife, Nancy, to arrange for his family and some of his students and colleagues to come to the Sullivan time station.

The Honey Badger poses with family, research group, and staff from the University of Illinois at TS 38 in Sullivan, IN. Such support provides a real morale boost to the racer.

There was another route detour before Sullivan, IN, and Greg was nervously watching a band of thunderstorms north and east on the radar. The detour had the worst pavement of the trip (not counting the gravel stretch in Colorado). Martin was terribly uncomfortable and asked repeatedly how much longer the rough pavement would last. It was slow going across the rough surface, but he finally made it and headed into Sullivan, where a large contingent of family and friends waiting excitedly for Martin to arrive. He stopped for ten minutes, took many photographs, and then headed on to Linton, IN where Ed settled Martin to sleep at the Park Inn.

Before Martin went to sleep, he discussed bike saddles with the crew. He was no longer comfortable on the Selle Italia SLK saddle on the TCR0, but he liked the Q-Labs saddles on the Merlin and the Superbike. Since Martin wouldn't need the Superbike much for the rest of the race, Greg swapped out the saddles on the TCR0 and the Superbike. Crew #1 arrived, and the bikes were piled into their vehicle. Greg changed the batteries in Martin's RAAM GPS at this point, since RAAM HQ had finally sent the instructions.

There were many signs in the Midwest for RAAM. Most of them were printed signs someone had put along the route, but others were handmade like this one.

After leaving Martin to sleep in Linton right on schedule (**keystone 2**), Crew #3 drove ahead to Lebanon, OH to stay at the Shaker Inn. They had stayed at a lot of mom 'n' pop places during the trip, and many of the owners and employees were interested in the event, but none like the woman at the desk at the Shaker Inn. She was very excited about the race and took notes on what was happening and the Honey Badger's website. Greg and Ed went out for a short run, took a dip in the pool, ran errands, and ordered 5-way chilis by walking through the drive-through at the Gold Star Chili. In Lebanon, Crew #3 also witnessed the most efficient Subway sandwich maker in the entire USA, and over the last week they had seen a lot of Subway sandwiches being made!

RACE DAY 9: June 22/23

The racer: Between Linton and Greensburg, IN, there is quite a bit of climbing in Brown County, but Martin was well-rested, and worked hard through the night on the Merlin without stopping (**keystone 3**). Martin rode through the silent night into Ohio. Oldenburg, Oxford (TS 41) and Blanchester (TS 42) passed, with some adventure: a major thunderstorm with tornadoes caught up with them, and Martin had to wait in the Expedition with Jay, Harry and Roy for an hour before it was safe again. At least Martin slept a half hour in the van while waiting, time that could be cut from the next sleep break. Amazingly, an 8-man team racer rode by in the storm. Stopping was a good call: the road was littered with fallen trees, mud slides, downed power lines and police officers barking at Martin when he got too close to the latter. So the home territory of Lee Kreider, who had done Martin's pre-race online interview, did not welcome him with good weather (see "The Ohio RAAM Show" on the internet). By this point, Martin had memorized the 237 songs on his iPhone navigation/entertainment device. The night's race ended in Chillicothe, OH, after 276 miles. By now, Martin was firmly in first place among the Masters, and he was approaching 6th place overall. Even during Martin's next sleep period, other contenders for the Masters title no longer managed to overtake him. Steady sleep and steady speed, while avoiding the hot mid-day, were beginning to pay off as day-riding took a toll among other racers, more of whom DNFd (**keystones 1-3**).

Driver Jay Yost, the Honey Badger and crew Chief Harry Zink are snapped by Crew #2 member Roy Tylinski while hunkering down near Oxford, Ohio to let a thunderstorm and tornadoes pass. They would soon be rerouted due to fallen power lines.

The crews: Crew #1 picked up Martin in Linton, IN, where he would begin some climbing. Julie had to switch out the wheel set on the Merlin, to a set Martin would need for some of the bigger climbs. The crews were getting very good at making sure they had the correct bikes for each stage of the race. Having three vehicles carrying different bikes at different times could have created major problems, but Martin had supplied everyone with a map of the US on when he would need each bike, and a second choice bike. This was extremely helpful and made switching bikes a smooth operation.

The Honey Badger walks across a mudslide in Ohio, as recommended by a RAAM alert.

Crew #2 picked up Martin for some more big climbing through Brown County. Jay was doing a lot of the driving now, and everyone was powered by his juicy beef jerky, including the racer. The TCRO, perfect for this area of mixed climbs and flats, by now had well-worn back brakes. Roy did his now-famous backseat acrobatics to replace the brake pads, but the new pads were rubbing the rim, and the cable had nothing left to give. Roy scraped down the brake pad with his utility knife, which had already saved more than one situation. Roy felt very sacrilegious. It was quite the feat to put the wheel in and out several times to check on the brakes in the back of the Expedition, but Roy was limber enough to get it done. No sooner did he finish when Martin stopped once again to swap bikes.

As Crew #2 rolled on through the darkness, they had to watch the weather. Major storms were looming in the north. A massive thunderstorm with a tornado warning eventually caught them, with such hard rain coming down that 3 crew members, 1 racer and 2 bikes were squeezed into the vehicle for an hour of napping to let the storm pass. During this time, the crew saw an intrepid 8-man team come through in dangerous winds, while Martin slept. Once the Honey Badger was back on the bike, he had to face the aftermath, which included dodging fallen trunks and rerouting around downed power lines. After the storm, Crew #2 handed off Martin to Crew #3 just after Miami University... in Ohio.

Crew #3 woke up after the same torrential storm, and discovered that Greg had left one of the rear car doors open. The car got wet inside, but fortunately nothing was missing. Martin had lost an hour waiting out the storm, so Crew #3 had to drive back to meet him at the exchange just outside of Oxford, OH. The aftermath of the storm had left many hazards on the road. At one point, Martin was riding directly toward a large branch in the middle of the road. Greg wondered, "He sees that, right? Surely, he sees that. Martin? Martin?!" As Ed honked a warning, Martin looked up (he had been looking at the GPS on his phone) and skidded to a stop. Shortly thereafter, there was a large mud slick that covered the entire road. Martin smartly opted to get off the bike and walk across it to avoid another close call.

Greg struggled to find a place for Martin to sleep between Blanchester and Chillicothe, OH. Crew #3 wanted him in bed no more than 21 hours after his last sleep (**keystone 3**). Fortunately, Martin finally had a stiff tailwind for the first time since Arizona, and he made great time across Ohio. Crew #3 got Martin to the Chillicothe Inn, which was just before TS 43. Martin liked checking off time stations before his rests, but this time Greg convinced him that it would save time to rest first. Martin wanted to cut his sleep to 3 hours, but Harry strongly discouraged it. When Martin learned of his Crew Chief's request, he gladly agreed to the full rest because he had pushed the envelope to make it to Chillicothe.

Greg did bike maintenance and sorted the red milk crates, while Ed relayed small maintenance issues to the other crews. Crew #3 then headed to Clarksburg, WV. Even though it was fairly late by the time they arrived, Greg went out for a run to get some much-needed exercise. He found a road to run on with a great name, "Benedum Run Rd," which seemed to say "Been a dumb run road."

RACE DAY 10: June 23/24

The racer: When Martin woke up in Chillicothe, he was in good spirits. His eyes were no longer red, his foot was feeling better in his old shoes, and Martin felt "strong" (i.e. able to do the planned 100 to 110 bpm on hills). From there, he proceeded to the most horrible stretch of the RAAM route: Highway 50 through West Virginia, where the shoulder is littered with large debris, yet the truck traffic is so dense one does not dare ride anywhere but on the shoulder during the day. Fortunately, Martin got through two thirds of it at night, and after Reynoldsville, he got off onto a more scenic side road before returning to a tamer Highway 50. Two hard climbs between Fellowsville and Oakland, MD concluded the day. Martin kept pace with an 8-man team climber, a good sign of strength after 2800 miles. In Oakland, he was about 6 hours ahead of the 2nd place Masters team, and 6th overall. It was time for an executive decision in consultation with Greg and Harry: Martin decided to sleep only 3 hours in the back of the van at the final rest stop, rather than bedding down for 4 hours at a motel as usual. This would safely keep him hours ahead of the #2 and #3 Masters racers. Although so little sleep would surely slow down the Honey Badger at the end, he was banking on making it through the huge Appalachian climbs before getting too fatigued.

The Honey Badger climbing towards Oakland, MD.

The three crews: Passing through Oxford, OH, the Golden Girls were asked to stop at the time station tent that had been damaged by the storm. The people there were hovering under their makeshift tent and appreciated praise for their commitment, despite extreme weather conditions. After picking up Martin in Chillicothe, they passed through Athens, OH late in the evening. Their best fan story happened in this town. As they headed into the town center, an oncoming cyclist began yelling "The Honey Badger, the Honey Badger!" He made a quick U-turn and pulled up to the driver's side of the van. He asked how Martin was doing and if we thought he would mind some company. He said, "It says in the rules I can ride alongside the racer for 15 minutes." Julie told him that Martin would love the company. The fan guided Martin through the small college town, through some rough brick pavement and a rocking bar scene. Martin enjoyed the friendly chat and soldiered on after saying goodbye to the rider after a few minutes. Martin was soon on a very busy highway and it was getting foggy. Lana had received warnings about a difficult construction area in Ohio, for which Crew #1 was advised to ferry the rider for about 4 miles in the back of the car if it seemed too dangerous to continue. Indeed, they reached the area late in the night and a cloud of fog had formed over the route. So they called RAAM headquarters, loaded Martin into the van and rode along the blocked-off road slowly with their lights flashing. This little break gave Martin a few minutes of binge eating time. Besides his regular snacks, he ate left-over pizza and trail mix. Never a dull moment with the Honey Badger.

Ed Scott washing Martin's race kit on June 24. This was a common duty during the race, as each crew had one main kit in their black clothing crate.

Just before the West Virginia border, Crew #2 picked up Martin in a nice thick fog. Thus began the dreaded 100-mile highway stretch on US 50. The first half during the night was quiet, just a few encounters with frogs and deer trying to take out Martin. They had to ferry Martin again per RAAM headquarters' orders, but with two bikes in the back there was no room for a third. So, with the rear window up, Roy sat in the back and held the last one over the bumper. Day broke, but the increasing traffic did not brake for Martin. It was shoulder-time to avoid a 70 mph rear-end collision. Zig-zagging around on the shoulder, Martin was avoiding tons of debris as the crew watched their mirror almost get knocked off by a passing truck. In the car, the crew talked to each other about bracing for impact to protect Martin. Luckily, the worst that happened to Martin on US 50 was a pinch flat and a lost tail light from bouncing around on swaths of rocks. Yet the obstacles were not over. The crew had to weave on and off the shoulder while Martin squeezed past construction signs on the right side. Once the crew got off US 50, they handed Martin off to Crew #3 and took a moment to breathe in nice and easy. The US 50 was the tensest part of the race for Crew #2.

Crew #3 drove back along the US 50 highway and set up for an exchange near East Salem. It had been drizzling through a thick fog. Martin asked to push the exchange a little further to get off of US 50, which he loathed. Ed drove ahead to onto SR98 and found a spot. Martin did a full kit change at the vehicle during the exchange (**keystone 4**), which prompted a comment from Jay, "You know, Martin, there are very specific rules about being naked." There was much traffic through little towns in West Virginia. Crew #3 largely used direct follow mode. Leapfrog was allowed, so they let Martin ride ahead while pulling off to let cars pass. The Honey Badger had a lot of tough climbing, with several fast descents. They saw many 4- and 8-person RAAM teams along the way, and there was a lot of camaraderie among the RAAM crews out on the road. Martin descended several miles at 9% with multiple hairpin turns. He stopped afterwards to let his hot rims cool down, to avoid blowing out a tire.

Crew #3 in action in their typical configuration with Ed driving and Greg working the route book, phones, and food/drink.

Martin was very hungry along the way, and enjoyed a flatbread BBQ pizza on the bike that the crew had bought at a sports bar. After he finished the pizza, he asked if they had anything sweet. Greg told him he would look around, and they dropped back. A few minutes later they saw an ice cream shop along the side of the road. Ed pulled off and Greg jumped out and bought a homemade ice cream sandwich. Martin woofed it down enthusiastically.

While Martin had not talked about the competition in the early stages of the race, he was asking about it regularly as they closed in on the finish. He had a lead of over 100 miles on his nearest competitor. Martin decided that he wanted to cut his last rest an hour short, skip using a motel, and sleep on a mat that they had purchased at a Wal-Mart a few days earlier. Crew #1 was sent ahead to find a spot for Martin to rest in Oakland, MD. When Crew #3 arrived, they pulled everything out of the Expedition, loaded it into the Crew #1 van, and quickly got Martin to rest in the back with the lift gate open. The crew agreed that they would wake Martin after three hours, or if his nearest competitor got within 50 miles, an intentional violation of **keystone 1** with one day of riding remaining.

Ed went with Julie and Lana to find lunch, while Greg went for a run. A massive thunderstorm forced Greg to duck for cover in a bathhouse. Greg then finished his run, and met up with the others in the parking lot. While at a KFC for lunch, the others were approached by a cyclist from the next time station, who was looking for Martin. The time station, was worried about Martin having gone off-course. While the crew had called RAAM HQ earlier to tell them that they were taking Martin off course, the local time station crew had not checked with HQ to learn this.

While discussing this in the corner of the parking lot, the crew heard knocking on the glass from the Expedition. Julie went over to find Martin pulling up his bibs, ready to ride. She told him that it had been less than two hours, but he responded, "90 minutes is a full REM cycle. Let's go." Greg asked him, "Did you actually sleep?" "Oh, yes, quite well." "Did you sleep through that thunderstorm?" "What thunderstorm?" The lift gate had been open during the heavy storm and the interior of the vehicle was wet right where Martin's feet had been, so he had clearly slept well! After Crew #1 left with the racer, Ed and Greg drove ahead to Hanover, PA for the night.

RACE DAY 11: June 24/25

The racer: Martin awoke after less than 2 hours, nervous about the lead. He had slept through a thunderstorm (very convenient timing), but a fly landed on his leg and woke him up. He was 4 hours ahead of #2, and not feeling bad, except for his chafed butt. Even Lanacane no longer provided complete relief. During the first crew shift, he got stuck in a street festival in the small town of Grantsville, and temporarily went into 5th overall, but only virtually: Robert Ferris got an even bigger time credit for getting stuck than Martin. The Honey Badger rode on to Cumberland with the Golden Girls. Then the hard climbing started: the most climbing per mile on the route, forget the Rockies. 6 major climbs awaited, but Martin had done most of them in 2013, and was mentally prepared. The Girls took him up #1, and then Jay & Harry & Roy took over for #2 through #6. Martin slogged up the mountains relentlessly, focusing on the demon in the pain cave, and finally won: he accelerated halfway through climb #4 and from then on, the climbs felt just fine, despite the pain in the butt. A slight rain did not deter Martin either, although he was cautious on the descents, so as not to end the race prematurely so close to the finish.

Martin with crew member Greg Scott and former graduate student Krish Sarkar near Mount Airy.

By the time the Honey Badger rode the rollers to Hanover, PA with Greg and Ed, he was coasting along "strong" (100 bpm). Rick Riley, another former Wild Card racer who had moved to the East Coast, greeted Martin along the route. It was noon, but there was going to be no sleep break today: only about 80 miles to the finish. But here the fatigue from just 2 hours' sleep on the last shift, then 0 hours this afternoon, took its toll. Martin was not able to push over the rollers on the superbike as planned, and Greg and Ed had to put him on the Merlin. At first he still coasted down the hills accelerating to take the next roller, but by Mt Airy (TS 52), Martin was crawling up the hills at ever dropping heart rate. 95…90…85…80… where would it end? Well, it ended at

75 bpm and 14 mph on the flats. To add insult to injury, a 10 mph headwind was blowing from the south. But second place was suffering even more, slowly falling back by 9 hours, and even the Male Open 'pros' had made it to the finish a day later than the usual 8.5 days. So Martin knew that he was actually in good position and in good shape. Egged on by Greg and Ed, and regular visits from Roy and Jay along the route, Martin plodded to Odenton in what seemed to take forever (but was probably just over 3 hours for the 40 miles). The heat and headwind amplified the fatigue, but Martin just went into Badger mode. He drank water when Greg rang a bell, like a Pavlovian dog; slogged through murderous climbs (really just 100 foot minor hills) at 6 mph; ate Belgian waffles; listened to Roy's encouraging shouts. Yet through all this, Martin always looked over his shoulder when changing lanes, and heeded the position of the crew vehicle, so clearly he was not terminally fatigued yet. No Shermer's neck here and still actively alert, while one of the Masters riders DNFd on the last stretch due to "mental fatigue." Another nice side effect: the body had become so numb that the persistent pain in the butt had vanished, and the ride felt like a slow Saturday morning group ride. For the last 9 miles after Odenton, Martin pulled out his earbud and just listened to Ed and Greg's directions while picking up small food items, eating more to pass the time than out of real hunger. Finally, General's Highway in Annapolis came into sight, and then the iconic Ram's Head Road House that marks the end of the road for the pain-stricken, dead-tired RAAM racer.

The Honey Badger switching cycling shoes during an enforced stop waiting behind a parade.

The three crews: Crew #1 made its way to Cumberland, MD and started the third of many climbs Martin would have to make through winding roads of the

Appalachian Mountains. There were a few pop-up storms which made the roads slick and hard to see. Out of all the shifts, this one made them the most nervous. With rain and other motorists cutting closely, it was a tense drive. They worried that the Honey Badger didn't get enough sleep, but after stopping for some rain gear, he seemed fine. They were sad, yet excited, to end their last shift, having almost completed one of the toughest bicycle races in the world. The Golden Girls would now make the drive to Annapolis and wait for Martin's finish.

Crew #1, Julie and Lana, at the Finish Line in Annapolis

As Crew #2 passed Crew #1 and Martin, they all got caught together right behind Robert Ferris (the eventual 5th place finisher) at a Founders' Day parade. They had some time to chat, and to load Martin up on the premium beef jerky that Jay had brought. They called in the delay, and RAAM Headquarters awarded time credits to everyone who was stuck. Once out of the parade, they sped up and down the Appalachian foothills until they found a nice meeting spot in a valley. Martin still had plenty of climbing left, and not the easy kind. Though this was no Wolf Creek Pass, there were many climbs. The gradients went up past 15% at a few points, real grinders, yet Martin miraculously managed.

The night through Maryland and Pennsylvania started smoothly for Crew #2, but then they missed a turn right before a gravel section that required ferrying the racer. Minimal time was lost getting Martin back on the route and ferried. He said he enjoyed the brief break in the van. Unfortunately, problems weren't over for Martin yet. Roy and Harry had forgotten to wash his drink bottles for a few days, and Martin's stomach was sensitive to the mold that had grown. After some back seat bottle washing by Harry, a quick restroom stop, and temporarily switching Martin to fresh bottles of unopened Mountain Dew for calories, it was an issue no more. Lesson learned. As the sun rose, Crew #2 passed the renowned Appalachian Trail, raced through some covered bridges, and across the storied battlefields of Gettysburg. Shortly thereafter, they left Martin in the hands of Greg and Ed for the final push into Annapolis. Crew #2 zipped ahead to check into the hotel in Annapolis, then Jay and Roy drove back on the route to cheer Martin on. Leapfrogging and cheering him as he passed, Martin was still as sharp as a razor, shouting out how many miles left each time. Roy and Jay then jumped ahead to the official finish line to catch the last of his RAAM.

The final crew exchange of the race, early morning of June 25th. The red tool and special clothing crates are visible in the Crew #3 van. Crew #2 member Roy Tylinski took the photo after moving the crates. Crew #2 driver Jay Yost (seen in the middle from the back) is attending the racer during the hygiene/jersey check. (The back of the Honey Badger's white jersey is just visible in the car door). Crew #3 member Dr. Ed Scott is watching over the operation on the right. See Figure 9.1 for a diagram of the exchange procedure.

Crew #3 had packed up in the morning to meet Crew #2 for the final exchange of the race, Greg's in-laws (who live outside Harrisburg, PA) showed up with a bunch of fig bars, which was a fortuitous gift as Greg had not been able to find any, and Martin would eat almost an entire box on the last day to the finish. The exchange with Crew #2 occurred just east of Gettysburg, and then they started toward the finish. After riding for a few hours on low sleep after violating **keystone 1** on the last day, Martin started to show heavy fatigue.

Crew #3 had to switch him to the Merlin because the climbing was too hard for a time trial position in his tired state. The 2nd place racer had fallen 9 hours behind, so the Honey Badger was almost certain to finish as the Masters champion.

While Martin had previously avoided stopping the bike whenever possible, doing all conversing while on the move, now Martin stopped several times on the side of the road. During one of these stops, Martin said to Greg "It's an interesting hallucination, but it seems like I have a stiff headwind." "Martin, there is actually a stiff headwind," Greg replied. At least our racer was only thinking he was hallucinating, not actually hallucinating. Several 4- and 8-person teams passed Martin in the last few hours, many offering him encouragement. At one point, an 8-man team crew vehicle pulled up and talked to Martin for a bit and Crew #3 overheard Martin say "Why? Because it's the Mount Everest of Cycling." They must have asked him why he was crazy enough to race RAAM solo.

The Blues Brothers Roy and Harry on the last race day, driving through the suburbs in Maryland on their way to Annapolis.

The finish The official finish line of RAAM is a piece of red tape between two cones. Voila. Martin rode across, and was greeted with a cold ginger ale by Roy, Jay, Ed and Greg (the other crew members had taken up position per instructions at the final hotel and near the official finish line). From there, they proceeded to a Shell station on Bestgate Road, where Martin wiped the grease off his legs with Armour-All wipes, changed into fresh kit and shaved, to feel somewhat like a human being again. The escort car drove him, Crew #2 and Crew #3 to the official finish line at the Annapolis Dock. He passed under the arch after being waved in by a volunteer. A crowd was cheering, including his sister Andrea, brother Philip, trainer Sarah, former student Krish Sarkar, and several other friends. Martin jumped on stage for his interview and a handshake from Head Official Jim Harms. Then Martin took photos with friends and family before heading to the hotel to meet up with the others before the banquet at 18:00.

Passing across the official finish line, followed by the Black Beast driven by Crew #3.

After getting stuffed with meat and beer at the banquet, the secretly hoped-for but never believed-in call to the podium came: Masters Champion of RAAM in 1st place, 9 hours ahead of 2nd place (who had not reached Annapolis yet), and 6th overall. Martin grabbed the microphone and shouted "The Honey Badger cares about one thing: I love my crew!" The Champion trophy is a nice wooden plaque of the US, with Oceanside and Annapolis marked on it. Never did the Honey Badger work so hard to win any award, bar none. Although, really, the award is immaterial at the end, a small symbol for all the suffering that can only serve as a palpable reminder of the race. Back at the hotel, Martin was barely able to stay awake while his crew recapped the race. Finally, Greg shooed him off to bed for 9 hours of sleep, his first real sleep in 11 days.

After 3089 miles, The Honey Badger had burned 80,000 calories and climbed 170,000 feet on the road to Masters victory in the "World's Toughest" ultracycling race. His crew had fed him about 220 HEED/Gatorade bottles, 100 gels, 80 bars, and 35 sandwiches. A large jar of Vaseline was depleted. 210 hours of music had played, from "Dark Side of the Moon" to Schubert's "Forellen Quartett." The Honey Badger fell asleep once on the bike. Three ferries through gravel, construction or oil on the road were necessary. Two rain- and thunderstorms, 800 miles of cross- or headwinds, and clothes changes atop a mountain pass with 30 °F wind chill on the descent challenged the racer and crew. Desert heat, inflamed eyes, sandstorms, fishtailing in gravel, falling off the bike and getting scraped up in Chillicothe did not stop the Honey Badger and his crew. Team Honey Badger made it in good time, 1.5 days behind the Open male winner, which is a strong Masters finish. Sometimes more is more: more regular sleep = more average speed.

The Honey Badger at the parade finish in Annapolis.

Honey Badger and Crew: Jay, Greg, Julie, Lana, Roy, Martin (holding the US-shaped Masters Champion trophy), Harry and Ed.

The 1st place Masters trophy, as a symbol of a lot of hard work by racer and crew spanning years of preparation and careful execution of the race plan.

13. RACE FINANCE

Although racer statistics and sleep cycles are more interesting than financial details, this book would be incomplete without some discussion of race finances. RAAM is expensive. In the best-case scenario, racers talk family into crewing, borrow vehicles from friends, and the crew sleeps on the side of the road. If all goes well, they come in significantly under $8,000 because of the hidden costs absorbed by family, friends and crew. In the worst-case scenario, racers come in from Europe with large teams of volunteers including medically trained personnel, renting vehicles and RVs, and paying plane fares and huge transportation fees. A budget up to $80,000 is not uncommon in that case.

The Honey Badger took an intermediate approach. All follow vehicles were rented to allow for quick replacement/roadside assistance. Crew and racer stayed at hotels. Expenses can be sorted into costs of a practice race (Chapter 6), pre-race expenses for travel to and stay in Oceanside, race expenses, and post-race expenses in Annapolis and on the way home. Table 13.1 on the next page briefly summarizes actual expenses for the Honey Badger's 2016 race, with some itemization so racers know what to expect for a 3000 mile crewed race.

Under item 4) for crew 3, the races expenses per crew are broken down some more. Each crew spent on average $2,350 during the race, about 40% for their hotels, another 25% for race vehicle fuel, 17% for crew and racer food, the rest for various supplies, ranging from batteries to a sleeping pad for the racer to sleep in the van on the last day of the race.

Although one can save money by relying on friends and family, we recommend the above approach. Insured rental vehicles are much easier to replace in case of an accident or malfunction, and less likely to fail. Hotel stays are much better for crew morale than sleeping on the side of the road or in a van.

Finances were organized as follows: The racer took care of all pre-race expenses, vehicle rentals, and post-race expenses. For the race, one member of each vehicle's crew was designated as the "Chief Financial Officer," or CFO. That person was pre-paid $1500, so they would draw on their own credit card during the race. That crew member made all major purchases during the race, settling any minor accounts with the other crew member. Post-race, they were then reimbursed *ca.* $850 per CFO to make up the shortfall from the $1500 pre-payment to the $2350 actual average expenses. Each CFO provided the racer with a complete set of scanned receipts or originals, plus a spreadsheet with data, type of expense, and dollar amount listed for each expense. This expectation was made clear before the race, and the CFOs tallied expenses very efficiently, within 2-3 days after the race was over.

Table 13.1 RAAM costs, including practice race, pre-race costs, race costs and post-race costs. Not included are bicycles purchased, in part, for the race.

1) Practice race:	
Three hotel rooms for racer and crew	$180
Small supplies and food	$80
Post-race dinner for racer and crew	$112
Rental van (crew vehicle)	$392
Fuel	$117
2) Pre-race receipts and reimbursements:	
RAAM race fee	$2950
Three rental vans	$3526
Crew transportation to race and related costs	$1717
Racer supplies (bike supplies such as multiple spare lights, Li batteries, tools; crew vehicle supplies such as amber lights and slow vehicle triangles; racer food; racer clothing, etc.)	$1885
Oceanside rental house	$1070
Pre-race dinner	$114
3) Race prepayments:	
Crew 1 CFO: Julie Turner	$1500
Crew 2 CFO: Roy Tylinski	$1500
Crew 3 CFO: Greg Scott	$1500
4) Race crew expenses (beyond the $1500 pre-pay):	
Crew 1	$605
Crew 2	$861
Crew 2 (Jay Yost, joined at TS 37 Effingham)	$352
Crew 3 (Typical breakdown for a single crew: $610 fuel; $350 crew food; $60 racer food; $915 hotels; $340 medicine, sleeping mat, supplies, batteries etc.)	$775
Racer hotels	$604
5) Post race expenses:	
Annapolis hotel	$941
Gas, for rental vehicle return	$210
Food, during vehicle return	$45
Extra RAAM banquet tickets	$190
6) Grand Total	$21226.00

Given the Honey Badger's experience, you may as well pre-pay your CFOs $2000 in 2016 dollars before the race. There was fairly little wastage in the receipts, most of it associated with panic moments: when the Honey Badger had red-eye coming out of Arizona, various crew members must have purchased a total of at least 6 bottles of medicated eye drops.

As a rough guide, if you

- rely on hotels before/during/after the RAW or RAAM,
- use rental vehicles,
- have 2-3 crew per vehicle,

then the cost for these races will be about $2700 per vehicle per 1000 miles in 2016 dollars.

14. AFTERWORD

We hope that the information in this book proves to be helpful to the aspiring solo RAAM Masters racer, as well as veterans of RAAM and ultra-endurance racing aficionados interested in studying various race strategies. There are many roads to a successful RAAM, but for the Honey Badger, the strategy outlined in this book was nearly optimal. With his strong circadian rhythm and inability to fall asleep at a moment's notice, the long-sleep, long-ride strategy with a break during the hottest part of the day was best. The crew for the 2016 race was much happier than the one for the 2013 race, and the reason is simple: fewer crew in more follow vehicles with shorter and more regular shifts were both busier, and got more rest. This avoided idle moments and strife, and still provided the necessary redundancy overall. It also simplified the entire race process into well-defined daily tasks unique to each crew, creating an efficient race flow and forward momentum that cannot be achieved with irregular scheduling.

If you have read this far, maybe you have wondered why Martin's cycling buddies call him the "Honey Badger." It's a story as silly as any nickname's. In 2012, the "Honey Badger Don't Care" video, in which a badger eats a cobra, gets bitten by a cobra, gets up again and eats another cobra, was going viral on YouTube. It so happened that in 2012 Martin visited Vietnam, where a cobra lashed out at him at a snake restaurant and he then ate it, much to the delight of his Vietnamese hosts. Later that year, Martin crashed 10 miles into an Ironman bike ride and broke two ribs. He got up, took some painkiller, finished the remaining 102-mile ride and marathon to complete the race, and then checked himself into the emergency tent for diagnosis. His cycling buddy Scott Dahman caught wind of the two incidents, and "The Honey Badger" it was: "Martin eats cobra/Martin falls/Martin gets back up on the bike/Martin don't care."

This is not a poetic or philosophical book, like Dex Tooke's RAAM adventure, but if the reader will indulge us, here is why our racer thinks he was motivated to do RAAM, whatever the real subconscious motives may have been. It's summed up in Chapter 12 with a question asked by an 8-man team crew out of a support vehicle window, and the answer the Honey Badger gave. "Why are you doing this crazy race, solo RAAM?" "Because it's the Mount Everest of Cycling." There are really two things that distinguish humans from other animals. Our intelligence, and our superb physical and mental endurance. Any yard dog can sprint 100 meters faster than Usain Bolt. Let's not even start on greyhounds and cheetahs. Michael Phelps' Olympic speed over 100 meters is sleepy cruising for a bottlenose dolphin. Of course there are also birds and whales that can migrate over large seasonal distances, greatly aided by winds and currents. But only humans have the willpower to direct their bodies to hunt a gazelle to exhaustion by following it over marathon distances. Only humans could execute a goal like riding 86,000 miles in a year (roughly the current annual mileage record, and beyond any migrating fowl or cetacean), running 135 miles across Death Valley, climbing the world's tallest mountains without extra oxygen, or covering 3000 miles in 10 days in a headwind going over every mountain, instead of around it. Even if another creature could physically do it, it would mentally fatigue long before reaching the goal. The will to endure is simply not strong enough, not even in most humans. That's why the crowd of multi-day ultra-endurance athletes is a small one. Long distance cycling is particularly appealing to the author because it marries our two unique abilities of intelligence and endurance: the bicycle is an artifact that sprang from the human mind, designed to amplify our natural physical ability mechanically, while still using only our own leg- and will-power. Ultracycling is a sport like ultrarunning or mountaineering. In mountaineering, technical accessories created by the human mind, like pitons, climbing shoes and ropes, are combined with the uniquely human endurance, willpower and deprivation tolerance (oxygen as well as sleep) to conquer Everest or the harder K2. Each year, about 40 well-trained people attempt K2, half to two-thirds succeed, and a few hundred in total have achieved the summit. RAAM has very similar statistics, although it is much safer, with a single-digit death toll in its decades of operation. More fatalities usually occur in a single year on K2. Perhaps there are endurance athletes even crazier than ultracyclists out there. And perhaps it is not entirely a coincidence that one of the 2016 RAAM solo racers came from Brixen, Reinhold Messner's home town in northern Italy.

15. BIBLIOGRAPHY

(1) Coyle, E. F.; Feltner, M. E.; Kautz, S. A.; Hamilton, M. T.; Montain, S. J.; Baylor, A. M.; Abraham, L. D.; Petrek, G. W. *Med. Sci. Sports Exerc.* **1991**, *23* (1), 93.

(2) Lahart, I. M.; Lane, A. M.; Hulton, A.; Williams, K.; Godfrey, R.; Pedlar, C.; Wilson, M. G.; Whyte, G. P. *J. Sport. Sci. Med.* **2013**, *12* (3), 481.

(3) Schumacher, Y. O.; Ahlgrim, C.; Prettin, S.; Pottgiesser, T. *Med. Sci. Sports Exerc.* **2011**, *43* (5), 885.

(4) Lahart, I. M.; Lane, A. M.; Hulton, A.; Williams, K.; Godfrey, R.; Pedlar, C.; Wilson, M. G.; Whyte, G. P.; SWAIN, D. P. *J. Sport. Sci. Med.* **2013**, *12* (3), 481.

(5) Galloway, S. D. R.; Maughan, R. J. *Med. Sci. Sports Exerc.* **1997**, *29* (9), 1240.

(6) Knechtle, B.; Wirth, A.; Knechtle, P.; Ruest, C. A.; Rosemann, T.; Lepers, R. *Chin. J. Physiol.* **2012**, *55* (2), 125.

(7) Dattilo, M.; Antunes, H. K. M.; Medeiros, A.; Monico Neto, M.; Souza, H. S.; Tufik, S.; De Mello, M. T. *Med. Hypotheses* **2011**, *77* (2), 220.

(8) Eastman, C. I.; Martin, S. K. *Ann. Med.* **1999**, *31* (2), 87.

(9) Oliver, S. J.; Costa, R. J. S.; Walsh, N. P.; Laing, S. J.; Bilzon, J. L. J. *Eur. J. Appl. Physiol.* **2009**, *107* (2), 155.

(10) Mougin, F.; Simon-Rigaud, M. L.; Davenne, D.; Renaud, A.; Garnier, A.; Kantelip, J. P.; Magnin, P. *Eur. J. Appl. Physiol. Occup. Physiol.* **1991**, *63* (2), 77.

(11) Lahart, I. M.; Lane, A. M.; Hulton, A.; Williams, K.; Godfrey, R.; Pedlar, C.; Wilson, M. G.; Whyte, G. P. *J. Sport. Sci. Med.* **2013**, *12* (3), 481.

(12) Belenky, G.; Wesensten, N. J.; Thorne, D. R.; Thomas, M. L.; Sing, H. C.; Redmond, D. P.; Russo, M. B.; Balkin, T. J. *J. Sleep Res.* **2003**, *12* (1), 1.

(13) Kuipers, H.; Keizer, H. A.; Brouns, F.; Saris, W. H. M. *Pflügers Arch. Eur. J. Physiol.* **1987**, *410* (6), 652.

(14) MacDougall, J. D.; Ward, G. R.; Sutton, J. R. *J. Appl. Physiol.* **1977**, *42* (2), 129.

(15) Potter, J. J.; Sauer, J. L.; Weisshaar, C. L.; Thelen, D. G.; Ploeg, H.-L. *Med. Sci. Sports Exerc.* **2008**, *40* (6), 1126.

(16) Geesmann, B.; Mester, J.; Koehler, K. *Int. J. Sport Nutr. Exerc. Metab.* **2014**, *24* (5), 497.

(17) Wishnofsky, M. *Am. J. Clin. Nutr.* **1958**, *6* (5), 542.

(18) Ivy, J. L.; *et al. Appl. Physiol.* **2002**, *93* (4), 1337.

(19) Ganio, M. S.; Klau, J. F.; Casa, D. J.; Armstrong, L. E.; Maresh, C. M. *J. Strength Cond. Res.* **2009**, *23* (1), 315.

(20) McLellan, T. M.; Bell, D. G.; Kamimori, G. H. *Aviat. Sp. Environ. Med.* **2004**, *75* (8), 666.

(21) Spriet, L. L.; Graham, T. E. Current comment from the American College of Sports Medicine: Caffeine and Exercise Performance http://www.acsm.org/pdf/CAFFEINE.pdf (accessed Aug 1, 2016).

(22) Burdon, C.; O'Connor, H.; Gifford, J.; Shirreffs, S.; Chapman, P.; Johnson, N. *J. Sports Sci.* **2010**, *28* (11), 1147.

(23) Goldstein, E. R.; Ziegenfuss, T.; Kalman, D.; Kreider, R.; Campbell, B.; Wilborn, C.; Taylor, L.; Willoughby, D.; Stout, J.; Graves, B. S.; Wildman, R.; Ivy, J. L.; Spano, M.; Smith, A. E.; Antonio, J. *J. Int. Soc. Sports Nutr.* **2010**, *7* (1), 5.

Made in the USA
San Bernardino, CA
04 January 2019